desert silence

A Way of Prayer For an Unquiet Age

Alan J. Placa & Brendan P. Riordan

Scripture quotations are from *The New American Bible* and *The Jerusalem Bible.*

Cover: Robert Manning

Nihil Obstat: Rev. George A. Denzer, S.T.D., Censor Librorum, 1977.

Imprimatur: Most Rev. John R. McGann, D.D., Bishop of Rockville Centre, 1977.

Published by: Living Flame Press / Locust Valley / New York 11560

ISBN: 0-914544-15-2

Printed in the United States of America

This book
is dedicated to
Alice and Pace Goldstein
with profound thanks
to God
for the gift of their friendship.

EPIGRAPH

"Abbot Lot came to Abbot Joseph and said, 'I keep my rule of life, I fast, I pray and meditate, and I maintain a contemplative silence. I do all of these things as well as I can in my own small way. As far as I can, I try to cleanse my mind of unwanted thoughts. Now, what more should I do?' The elder stood up to answer, and he stretched out his hands towards heaven, and his fingers became like ten lamps of flame. He said, 'Why not be totally changed into fire?' "

Verba Seniorum,
The Sayings of the Desert Fathers

CONTENTS

PREFACE

The desert is a harsh place. It can be cruel and uncaring, its hot and unsympathetic breath easily overcoming the unwary traveller. But this same desert also offers its own valuable and unique reward: its silence.

Which of us could not at some time in his life envy the ancient Fathers who went out to the desert seeking that silence? Even when we imagine or try to feel the oppressiveness of that scorching heat, the bitter thirst and the pangs of hunger, do we not still sense that theirs was a life we could willingly embrace? Or, as the cares and pressures of daily living mount, is it not sometimes attractive to picture oneself in the dark, cool cloisters of some great abbey, lost in a community of believers offering themselves totally to God?

We secretly envy the ancient Fathers and the monks of our own day for many reasons. Cynics today would say that the flight to the abbey or desert is nothing more than an escape from the responsibilities of our demanding world and style of life. Gibbons levelled much the same charge at the typical Desert Father when he described him as "... a hideous, distorted, and emaciated maniac, without knowledge, without patriotism, without natural affection, spending his life in a long routine of useless and atrocious self-torture, and quailing before the ghastly phantoms of his delirious brain, which had become the ideal of the nations that had known the writings of Plato, and the lives of Socrates and Cato."

If we are to dare to see these men and women of the desert as guides for our own spiritual quest, then we must be willing to admit the truth of at least a part of this criticism; but we must also be ready to transcend the critique and ultimately to reject it as an insufficient indictment of what the Fathers went out to find.

The universal fascination which the cruel but quiet desert holds for men and the lure of the dark but consoling monastic enclosure are a flight from reality — but what a reality it is that they flee! It is the reality of the overburdened, the aimless, the useless, squandered energy of our times — a reality which laughs back at us and mocks us with the final knowledge that all we have expended of ourselves in search of the world's peace makes little difference. The flight to the desert must begin with the painful confrontation with this truth: that I am daily dying in pursuit of things which are not only dead themselves, but whose deadly possession further kills the spirit which thirsts for a more permanent life. This beginning, this first confrontation, is the easiest step of all. It takes only very little serious reflection to wish for something better.

That first step is made by any man who perceives that human society has always presented comfort, pleasure, and temporal security as goals, and yet has always failed to quench man's thirst for lasting peace. The second, heroic step begins with reflection on what we have secretly known all along: that deep within ourselves, none of us wants to be "society's child"; none of us wants to seek the imposed goals of a world that kills us in its own mad chase after self-destruction. Once we accept ourselves as integrally belonging to the *real* world of nature, as brothers and sisters of creation, we begin to search for a way in which we can live at peace here in our home. We begin to see that so much of our effort to survive has been an attempt to make us stronger and more secure in our own environment. Life is not a battleground, a war with all that is around us; it is not even merely a peaceful coexistence with nature. It is to be a harmonious union of myself, my own being, with all that God has created.

Just as we each sense this striving within ourselves, this striving for the resolution of conflict and union with God's creation so, too, did the Desert Fathers. But rather than engaging in vain meditation upon their unique and personal place in nature, rather than giving themselves over to occasional exercises in self-awareness, the Fathers saw the re-establishment of their relationship with creation as critical for their very existence and their spiritual survival and growth.

The intellect may reject all of this as containing nothing new, and yet our experience of being in the world makes us crave more. We feel we are accomplishing nothing, and so we crowd our hours with more and more work. We are overcome with boredom and a sense of the futility of our lives, and yet we cram in more soap operas, more forgettable best-sellers, and more momentary thrills of violence and sex at the movie theater. We complain that we are tired of the other-worldly dogmas of established Christianity and then succumb to the fascination of "pop cults" and instant spiritual experiences. Our personal relationships seem to be going nowhere and to bring us less and less satisfaction, and we turn to "meditation" and to drug trips that take us so far into ourselves that we have no time or room for those whom we seek to love.

The Desert Fathers were probably as tempted as we are to see the problem and reject the obvious cure; but they recognized the Physician who was needed, and they knew how they must find Him. They knew they must commit themselves radically and completely to the Lord.

We are not suggesting that life can have no meaning unless a man abandons his life completely and flees to the desert. The Fathers themselves never counselled that. They never dared to say that their way was the only way to salvation: they only knew that the heroism of that way made the path to salvation clear for themselves. In retrospect, we know that their having travelled that radical path has made the way clearer for us. Our task in this book will be to uncover the rich spiritual legacy they have left for us. What is important for us today is *who* they were, *what* they did, and *why* they succeeded in finding the Lord.

Are we really so very different from these men and women of the desert? They were the most ordinary and the most extraordinary of men, a cross section of any society. They were oppressed by the same vexing questions and the same profound choices we face today. They differ from us only in that they took that radical, heroic second step: they not only speculated on what they might be able to do to change themselves, but they faced the challenge to do all that might be necessary to come to an understanding of who they were and why they existed.

These were honest men, perhaps more honest than we. They rebelled against a world they felt was alien and trying to direct their lives away from the Truth. Their first step in rebelling against the moral suffocation of that world was to recognize personal evil in their lives. It is difficult to isolate and identify the forces and pressures that lead a man to evil, but surely the situation of the Fathers was not so different from our own. We often condemn the twentieth century as a secular society, as the final age in sensuality, in faithlessness, and in violence. But human history has rarely revealed ages either profoundly better or profoundly worse than our own. The Roman Empire would hardly blush at our immoralities, at our confused and disjointed religious culture, and could hardly be revolted by our excesses of brutality and insensitivity. Our only claim to have surpassed Rome is in the means of degradation at our disposal, rather than in any greater capacity for degradation.

We can certainly match the Desert Fathers in abhorrence for the sin and weakness around us, if only we will open our hearts to God's Law and His promise of life.

I. The World Of The Fathers

Some sort of renunciation of the world has been part of the Christian vocation from the very beginning. Jesus was called to be the Christ from the beginning of time, and He sensed the need for a purifying renunciation from the beginning. St. John tells us that "In the beginning was the Word" (*John 1:1*) and that "not one thing had its being but through him" (*1:3*). From the first moment of creation He was pouring Himself out for us.

It is true to say that the Desert Fathers renounced the world, but it would be shallow to say that they gave it up, or that they left it. Giving something up is an act of the will, and leaving something is a motion of the body. Renunciation is a posture of the heart. It is not clear that the Fathers set out to imitate Christ in their renouncing of the world — in fact, a literal imitation of Him would have kept them in society as He had always been — but they ended up by catching one of the fundamental rhythms of His heart, and they found their sanctity in that more profound imitation.

In reaching out for glory with His Father, Jesus let His earthly life slip away. It was not by chance or from distraction that it slipped away, but rather as the final and most radical admission that no man can ever express the full meaning of his life in his bodily living. A man may die by accident, but death itself is not an accidental part of human living. In his *Life of Christ* Bishop Fulton J. Sheen says that "the cross of Calvary cast its shadow over the manger of Bethlehem." In that dramatic *phrase* we are reminded that human life has the stamp of death on it. For those without faith or hope this is a morbid prospect because it is a fearsome reminder of the fragility of our biological life.

For the man of faith, for the man convinced that each moment of life is a potential opening to new growth and new life, however, there is less fear. The inevitability of death is a reminder that man faces one final and totally recreative opening to new life. For the "believer" whose imagination is closed, this expectation makes earthly life less than valuable because it is only a testing through which we must impatiently suffer. For the mature Christian, the hope of ultimate transformation is a horizon against which he sees each moment of earthly life as a new opportunity to know, and to believe, and to love, and to hope more deeply. The man who would live with his hands outstretched, ready to receive new gifts of life at every moment, must be a man prepared to relinquish what he has already known, and believed, and loved, and hoped for because of his radical openness to God's promise. That is the posture of renunciation; that is the attitude of Christ "lifted up" on the cross, Christ who relinquished and renounced His earthly life that He might ascend to glory and that we might have life more abundantly.

The story is told of one of the Desert Fathers who sold his precious copy of the Gospels and gave the money to a poor man and said, "I have sold the book which told me to sell what I had and give it to the poor."

But the Fathers did not go to the desert because they had already learned what it would mean to renounce all for Christ. That mystery was their unexpected reward, not their plan. They went out at first prompted by a vaguer and simpler uneasiness with the world around them. From their point of view, Christianity had been most vigorous when imperial persecution had made the "cost of discipleship" a clear thing. The new age of peace that had begun with the Edict of Milan in A.D. 311 and the reign of the Emperor Constantine (A.D. 312-337) made being a Christian an easy thing, a thing without great price.

What was even more distressing, the new respectability of Christianity put Christians into more intimate contact with the values of the world. The Gospel's value system, the promise of eternal life, and the call to spiritual perfection had now to compete with the promise of earthly paradise offered by the merchants and politicians of secular society.

What the Fathers renounced at first was the tangible and visible comfort that seemed to hold them back from growing. Gnawing at them, deep inside, was the suspicion that there could be more to life, more strength in themselves, more faithfulness and openness to God. They were not already saints who were suddenly distracted from their sanctity by secular culture: they were ordinary men, in some cases plain and even coarse men, whose imaginations had been teased by the Gospel.

Their experience is pertinent to our situation precisely because we find ourselves in very much the same predicament. Our concern is not for saints who are occasionally tempted by the world; it is for ordinary Christians whose first steps in faith and in prayer are made nearly impossible by the noise, the triviality, and the rootlessness around them.

To understand correctly what the Fathers were renouncing we must have at least a simple understanding of the society in which they lived. To understand why the attempted marriage between Imperial Rome and the Church of Christ frightened them we must understand the moral strength which brought Rome to its greatness, and the moral decay which brought it to its crisis.

THE MORAL STRENGTH OF ROMAN SOCIETY

When we think of ancient Rome we visualize the splendor of the empire, and it is hard for us to conceive of the simple beginnings. We don't think of the town of Rome and its surrounding province of Latium struggling for survival on a hostile peninsula. It is hard for us to imagine the suffering and the determination of simple farmers fighting to make their lands safe. And yet those are the beginnings of Rome — lost, and yet glorified now in legend and poetry. The first Romans were austere people of simple virtue. They loved their families and their lands; they loved their gods and their cults; they had a thirst for orderliness and strength and security.

They summed up these plain virtues in the single word *pietas*. The force of their *pietas* drove them to secure their lands and, eventually, to bring peace and order to the whole Italian peninsula. After generations of sacrifice they had reached a plateau: protected by the Mediterranean and by the Alps, Roman Italy seemed ready to rest and to live in peace and *pietas*.

THE DANGERS OF PEACE

But rest is an ambiguous reward for bitter struggle. Some men grow soft and lazy when left to rest; others grow restless and discover new horizons in themselves and seek new adventures.

In order to secure peace in the peninsula, the army had built roads and protected them. In order to defeat the challenge of Carthage the Romans had made the Mediterranean *Mare Nostrum*, "Our Sea." Romans who found security a stultifying state turned to commerce and used the roads and sea to make a profit in satisfying the new and more sophisticated tastes of their countrymen.

The empire began as a network of protected

trade routes that carried luxury goods to the prosperous citizens of Rome. But peace and luxury were already exacting their price. Austerity and determination are not virtues associated with luxurious living. By the time of Christ there was already a reaction against this growing softness. Julius Caesar was a man of the old *pietas*, and his adopted son, Octavian, the first emperor, inspired and patronized high art to sing the praises of the ancient virtues and the ancestral gods.

AN EMBARRASSMENT OF RICHES

But the weakness had gone too far, and the lure of the exotic was already too strong in Rome. The restless hearts of idle men and women hungered for novelty, and the vastness of the empire brought them an endless supply of new spices, new fabrics, and new faiths. From the East came the "mystery cults" of Egypt, the Judaism of Palestine with all of its countless sects, and the newest and most bizarre of the Jewish sects: a group who worshipped a crucified carpenter.

The Roman Empire was vast and rich and well organized, and so its mortal illness lingered for three centuries, but its death was inevitable. It required immense complacency, executive incompetence compounded by palace intrigues and assassinations and military coups, a disastrous plague, several periods of catastrophic inflation, and an endless stream of foreign or "barbarian" intruders but, finally, Rome did fall.

When Constantine embraced the Church his generosity was due, at least in part, to his desire to rebuild the empire around a new moral core which could fill the vacuum left by the disintegration of the old values and virtues of Rome. In Constantinople, the "New Rome" of the East, Church and empire began together and the marriage lasted a thousand years beyond Constantine. In the West, the momentum of decay was too far gone, and the empire was dead in a hundred years.

A FIRST RENUNCIATION

The Desert Fathers sensed more than political decay, though. They had a far more fundamental doubt about the possibility of a "Christian State." They were not Greek philosophers; they were simple *fellahin* of Egypt, and they feared that the respectability of Christianity would make renunciation an apparently unnecessary thing.

They began their search for pure gospel living in an exuberant and even childish way. They fled to the desert to escape respectability and peace as Christians had fifty years before to escape persecution and death. Those whose vision never grew beyond that first enthusiasm were lost in the desert. Those whose hands and hearts were open, who were ready to relinquish and renounce their own goals in favor of God's, found life and real peace.

II. The Spiritual Journey Of The Fathers

Christians first began going out to the Egyptian desert around the year A.D. 250. That year is a significant turning point in the history of the empire. For Christians in particular it was significant because it marked the beginning of the first general persecution of all Christians in the empire. But it was also the beginning of a disastrous period for the whole world. Around A.D. 250 a plague struck which extended from Palestine to Britain. The many deaths which resulted reduced the work force considerably. Because of the scarcity of manpower, much fertile land was unworked, and the resulting poor crop drove food prices upward. The government responded by devaluing the silver currency to such an extent that at one point it contained less than two per cent silver.

This combination of religious persecution, disease, and economic chaos made life within the empire seem completely intolerable for many, especially many poor Christians in Egypt. They fled to the desert surrounding the city of Thebes (which is called the Thebaid) and to another wilderness area called Scete. The Fathers of whom we are speaking came to the desert nearly a hundred years later, and yet it is important to speak of this first flight for two reasons. First, some permanent establishments were created in the desert around A.D. 250. Some holy men did establish themselves in the desert in those early days. Although they lived solitary lives they attracted disciples, younger men who wished to observe and imitate the holy men. In some places, then, a certain tradition of desert living for the sake of holiness had been established as early as A.D. 250.

Second, and we think more important, that earlier spiritual exodus exercised an imaginative power over Christian people, especially the Christians of Egypt and Palestine. When the crisis of the fourth century came along, when the new peace between Church and empire seemed to threaten the vitality of Christianity, men and women were prepared to see the desert as a symbol of austere and dedicated gospel living.

We ought to begin our examination of the experiences of the Desert Fathers with answers to some very simple questions. We have already answered two simple questions: "Where and when did they go?" They went to the Thebaid and to Scete, small numbers at first, around the year A.D. 250, and then many more after the beginning of Constantine's reign in A.D. 312. Two additional practical questions suggest themselves: "What did they do in the desert?" and "Who were they?"

LIFE IN THE DESERT

We should start off our answer to the first of these questions by making an obvious point: they worked very hard. Simply to survive alone in a wild place is a difficult job, and the Fathers had to face that difficulty. Where possible, they tended vegetable gardens to supply what they needed for their meager diet. In order to earn money for the things they couldn't grow, they also engaged in simple forms of "cottage" manufacture, like basket weaving; they would collect the materials and spend long hours plaiting baskets, and then they would carry their work to market. Also, they had to build and maintain their own crude shelters. Though we think of them correctly as people of prayer, it would be a mistake to imagine they had the luxury of a great deal of free time for formal and elaborate prayer. Their practical situation demanded that they engage in hard, physical work. They were extremely poor people, struggling against a harsh and hostile setting to stay alive.

Another thing which occupied their energy and attention was what we can call "fasting." That seems an odd thing to say, since we think of fasting as a matter of *not* doing something. In fact, their fasting was a somewhat more complicated matter; it was an expression of a general, ascetical attitude. The Fathers were concerned with simplifying bodily living, purifying it and freeing themselves from trivial luxuries so as to prevent their bodies' wants from dominating their spiritual needs. We will have a great deal more to say about the asceticism of the Fathers in the next chapter, but it is important now to note that this fasting was part of what they did in the desert.

It may seem unnecessary to point this out, but a great deal of the Fathers' time was spent in prayer. Again, we will be examining this in greater detail later on, but for now we must observe that all of this prayer was connected with the sanctification of the routine of their lives. The psalmist says, "Seven times a day I rise to praise You," and the Fathers took this prescription literally. Building their prayer around the hundred and fifty Psalms and readings from the Scriptures and various liturgical hymns, they sanctified the hours of their days and their nights by praying to God and praising Him. This is the root of the "Divine Office" or "Liturgy of the Hours" which is still a keystone of the Church's liturgical life today.

We also believe, from their writings, that they had regular Eucharistic celebrations. They have left us no detailed descriptions of these, and so it is difficult for us to say precisely how they participated. Few of them were priests, and it is not clear how or where they got to Mass. And yet in their letters and written sermons and commentaries on Scripture they speak beautifully of the Eucharist.

Finally, they also prayed in a more private and less formal way. From simple ejaculatory prayer, like "the Jesus prayer" and the recitation of short Scripture passages while at work, to deep periods of contemplation, they prayed constantly. It is our ultimate purpose in this book to speak about the conditions and predispositions necessary for us to imitate their life of prayer: the formal sanctification of the hours, the deep love of the Eucharist, and their silent prayer of the heart.

One final point must be made about what they did in the desert, and that is to raise the question of their attitude toward study and intellectual activity. It is clear that at first the Desert Fathers had a distinctly anti-intellectual bias. Those who came to them for spiritual counsel were forbidden to read any book but the Bible, and they were discouraged from questioning the Scriptures or taking an intellectual approach to them.

As time passed, however, and as life in the desert matured and became a recognized path to Christian holiness, this anti-intellectual bias dissolved. To be sure, the Fathers always retained a certain healthy cynicism about the dilettantes of the world, but many of them became serious scholars and great writers.

By the middle of the fourth century it would be fair to say that the typical "monk"* of the desert spent his time in an orderly round of physical labor, fasting and ascetical practices, prayer of various kinds, and study of the Scripture combined with serious reflection on the theological issues of the day.

Before moving to the question "Who were

*We will be using the word "monk" as a more precise name for all of those who went out to the desert. "Monk," from the Greek word *monos*, meaning "one," refers to one who lives a solitary life. The designation "Desert Father" should be used to designate only the great saints and spiritual masters of the desert.

they?" we would like to say a word about "hospitality" in the desert. When speaking about men who lived an essentially solitary life in the wilderness it would seem strange to mention hospitality, but it was an important characteristic of their life. Of course, they followed the gospel injunction to offer hospitality to the occasional traveller in their neighborhood, but there was more. The monks themselves spent some time travelling regularly. They visited one another to pray together, to seek help and spiritual direction, to hear news of their friends, and to learn to grow in prayer and holiness. We mention this here because it points to another aspect of the monk's life: each of them was a student and a teacher in the desert's school of holiness.

CONVERSION AND RE-FORMATION

What sort of experience could be powerful enough to lead a man to abandon his life in the world and flee to a deserted wasteland? Answering this important question hardly requires subtle investigations of religious psychology. At least at the outset, the Fathers' motivation was quite simple: they had heard the gospel message, and it had moved them and shown them a high ideal; they sought an undefined deepening of their relationship with God, their Creator and Savior; they believed that their society was basically uncongenial to their search for God; and finally, and perhaps most directly, they had experienced a deep sense of remorse for their own personal sins.

Perhaps more important than questioning their

first motivation is asking what it was that compelled these strange men to remain in the seemingly hostile environment of the desert. We believe that they remained because in taking the risk of attempting a thorough, personal moral change and in taking the risk of drawing closer to the Lord, they discovered something far more powerful than their own efforts at conversion. They discovered the power of the Holy Spirit at work in them to change the very quality of their lives.

"The Spirit, too, comes to help us in our weakness. For when we cannot choose words in order to pray properly, the Spirit himself expresses our plea in a way that could never be put into words" (*Romans 8:26*).

In discovering that power of the Spirit they made a second, more painful discovery. They found that far beyond the wound of their personal sins they were also alienated from God, from the world of nature around them, and from their very selves. At the same time, this knowledge brought joy: they had discovered the power of the Holy Spirit which was available to them because of Christ's redemption and because of their Baptism into His redeeming death. They had discovered that the power of Baptism enabled them to gather together the elements of man's shattered integrity and to re-form those elements into the harmonious whole God intended man's life to be.

In the desert they found that "unity which has the Spirit as its origin and peace as its binding force" (*Ephesians 4:3*). They did not go out to create new order, or new structure, or new communities; they went out to find the peace, the harmony, and the natural rhythms of God's creation which would uncover for them the true unity which is the heritage of all those who have the Spirit from their Baptism.

Our reason for questioning the motivation of the Fathers is our interest in locating the same feelings in ourselves. If we can find the same needs in our hearts, then perhaps we can find the same strengths. But searching for their motivation is essentially an investigation in religious psychology, and we are hampered in the search by a lack of information. Our twentieth-century minds are accustomed to thinking in terms of psychological motivation, but the biographers of the Fathers did not think in such terms. We have to piece together an understanding of the Fathers' motives from our understanding of the world in which they lived, from what they have written, and from the "Sayings of the Fathers" that have been preserved and handed down to us.

One thing which is certainly common to all the Fathers is a sense of repentance for sin, and any insight into their motives for seeking perfection must begin with an insight into the reality and meaning of personal sin. Personal sin is an unpopular notion in the world today, and its unpopularity is one of the symptoms of the fact that we are badly in need of the kind of conversion of which the Fathers speak. We have been conditioned all of our lives to look at ourselves in very extreme terms. On the one hand we are invited to look at ourselves and at our consciences as the only real way of evaluating right and wrong in our lives. On the other hand, we are constantly reminded that the project of being alive is so overwhelmingly complex that no one person could ever have complete control of it himself.

The first piece of conditioning makes it easy for us to sin, because it makes us a law unto ourselves. The second makes it easy for us to absolve ourselves of guilt for our sins because we can't really be held responsible for the mistakes that we make under the tremendous pressure of modern living.

The advertising media have left all the meanest and least significant choices in life to us: "What will I eat?" "What will I wear?" "How will I smell?" But the truly important decisions belong to someone else, to "them." We have placed all our trust in institutions outside of ourselves, in complex technologies which we imagine can grasp and solve the problems of modern living. We have been radically alienated from what is most important because we have been willing to give up the effort to deal with the significant in favor of expending all of our energies on the trivial. We have a tremendous stake in the institutions and social constructs around us because of what we have invested in them: our independence, our individuality, and our humanity itself.

Sin is an alien concept in our world because it implies that a man is free enough, powerful enough, and creative enough to do something which can profoundly affect his own life. Our society bombards us with excuses for being half human, weak, and sinful. There is no personal responsibility, only "corporate" and "social" guilt. In the face of the vastness of society and the complexity of life we are all so puny and small, so insignificant, that nothing that happens is ever really our own fault. In a world view like ours, sin is not forgiven; it is lost in the shuffle. Original sin, the guilt of the human race, has been inflated until it has burst: we believe so deeply in our common guilt that we no longer acknowledge our individual failures. Original sin has been expanded to the point where it is general enough to apply to everyone yet not specific enough to apply to anyone.

The Fathers, living in a world that was simpler than ours, sensed their own personal sin and guilt, and they went to the desert to slough off all of their society's excuses for weakness. They did not want to escape human society; they only wanted to leave behind them all of the trivial things society says are the proof of our worth. They wanted to cut themselves off from what is false and designed only to produce superficial security, so that they could find their real, fundamental worth.

The same temporizing which makes me absolve myself from guilt also cuts me off from my potential for growth and achievement. "It is not the healthy who need the doctor, but the sick" (*Matthew 9:12*). The first step towards holiness is the recognition of sin, the recognition that we need the power of the Lord to heal us. If a man cannot look at his actions and see that they have caused suffering to himself and to other people, that they have damaged his relationship with God, then he will have no need for Him.

If our image of what we must do is simple enough to be grasped completely, if all of our goals are attainable by our own strength, then we will have no need for God. We will be like the Pharisee in the Temple. That man was a profoundly good man: he was generous, prayerful, studious, and devoted to his religion. He saw his goals clearly, and he had achieved them at the cost of much sacrifice and hard work. But they were *his* goals. He asked nothing of God and he received nothing. "And when you pray, do not imitate the hypocrites: they love to say their prayers standing up in the synagogues and at the street corners for people to see them. I tell you solemnly, they have had their reward" (*Matthew 6:5*). The man who knows he is sinful, who hardly knows how to begin to improve, who only knows he must turn to the Lord and beg forgiveness is the man who has made a sound beginning in faith.

But that sort of repentance is only a first step. Real reformation of life has to follow from it. The simplest reformation which is required is reformation which leads us away from our sinful acts and brings us to a style of living marked by virtue. But a still deeper re-forming of life must also come. Sin is a shattering experience because it cuts a man up into so many pieces: it allows each part of a man to run wild and seek its own satisfaction. A man's pride begins to have a life of its own, and does and says things of which the man's common sense would never approve. His passions are independent of his modesty; his anger and his self-righteousness never consider his need to be loved and cared for.

And the process of excusing ourselves for our own faults divides us still more. The will becomes an impotent stranger which can do nothing about our actions; it has no responsibility and we begin to look at ourselves as constant victims of "forces" greater than ourselves. At every moment we are divided and subdivided, alienated from our own feelings and our own powers. We become exhausted by our own failures.

The Desert Fathers sought real re-formation of their lives. They believed deeply that all men are called to holiness, that the image of God is in man, and that a man could reassemble all of his alienated parts into a harmonious whole. They were profoundly committed to integrity: to man's internal integrity, to the integrity of human relationships, and to the integrity of the relationship between God and man. They were concerned with saving themselves from the fate of men in the world: the fate of being reduced to spiritual impotence in exchange for false security, and a sense of comraderie with others who lack the courage to admit their guilt and to aspire to holiness.

THE COST OF DISCIPLESHIP

During the Second World War, a German Protestant theologian named Dietrich Bonhoeffer wrote a book called *The Cost of Discipleship*. He raised his voice from the midst of the hopeless sufferings of a German concentration camp, and he knew the cost of discipleship intimately. At a time when men were discovering the depths to which the human spirit could sink in degradation, Bonhoeffer spoke of the heights to which man could rise in love for his brothers and in hope in God.

It is a commonplace observation that in times of profound danger men find new strength and courage in themselves, whereas in times of relative comfort, a kind of complacency creeps over the human heart. The Church was born in suffering, and she has experienced her greatest moments in times of suffering. Over the main altar of the chapel at the seminary where we teach there is a group of figures that depict the crucifixion and birth of the Church. Christ on the cross is the central figure, and He is flanked by Mary, His Mother, and by St. John. Out of Christ's pierced side there flows a stylized stream of water which swirls round to Mary and to John. The Church was born as He shed His Blood, and as that water of life flowed from His side.

It was in this ultimate act of renunciation, in this moment when Christ faced death, "a death He freely accepted" as the Roman liturgy says, that the union of God and man was fully perfected. Christ's quiet obedience to the will of His Father brought Him to glory and opened the way to glory for us. The very first generation of Christians suffered social ostracism and imprisonment, and they were strengthened by that suffering. There could be no doubt about the cost of the Faith: if one were to be a follower of Christ, it would mean renouncing much of the life one had known previously.

That suffering did not diminish for the Church; rather it increased as time passed. By the year A.D. 250, when the Roman persecution was in full swing, the cost of faith was clearer still. Anyone who wished to be a Christian had to face the realistic possibility that the proclamation of the Faith could cost him his life. This age of martyrs was an age when the Church grew and flourished enormously. As St. Ignatius, Bishop of Antioch in the third century, travelled under arrest to Rome where he was to be executed for the Faith, he wrote to the churches along the way thanking them for their kindness and praising God for the fate he was about to face. Finally, as he approached Rome itself, he wrote to the Roman Christians and asked them not to interfere in his case, not to try to intervene on his behalf. He explained to them that he had always understood that the commitment to the Faith was a commitment of one's entire life, and that he was now ready to pay the price of that commitment. To us the story seems deeply romantic, and Ignatius' courage seems immense. And yet he does not describe himself as a man of great courage. He sees himself simply as a man of common sense. It seemed logical to him that anything worth the conversion of one's life could someday be worth one's life itself.

This is the essential posture of the Desert Fathers and the key to the style of prayer their experience suggests. They were men who, like the martyrs before them, had grasped the immense cost of Christian discipleship. When they began to hunger for a deeper awareness of the power of God, when they sensed their own need for "something more" than the world could offer, they determined to throw themselves completely into the world which God had created. They made this leap of faith because of a profound conviction which they held: that the secret of God's life was before them, available to their hearts, if only they could reintegrate themselves into the natural world He had created and the natural laws He had established for it.

Modern man feels that hunger no less, and yet he makes totally different choices. It is said over and over again that young people today are open to faith because they know the need for transcendence in their lives and in the world. It has become almost a magical incantation to say that there is great hope for religion in the modern world because so many people are interested in mysticism and meditation and Eastern spirituality. It is as if by saying those words we can exorcize the demon we all fear. And here is the demon: that religion is being trivialized; that faith and feeling have been hopelessly confounded; that fashionableness will be the death of religion as surely as it has been the death of every other fad it has seized in its commercial hands.

Modern man certainly feels the same hunger the Desert Fathers felt, but rather than following their example and inserting himself radically into the world, modern man has chosen to divorce himself more and more from reality. There are two basic streams of mysticism in world religions. One, the Western stream, is a tradition which we may call "incarnational." The Desert Fathers are distinctly within this stream insofar as their spirituality imitates God's method of offering Himself to man.

The history of Judaeo-Christian revelation is not a history of flashes of insight. For every second of blinding revelation like that to Saul on his way to Tarsus, there are centuries of quiet unfolding of the mystery of God's life. For every page of the Book of Scripture there are scores and scores of years which are the "pages" of the book of nature into which God has written the Truth about His ways.

When God chose to reveal Himself to man — and only He knows why He made that choice — He chose to do it in a gradual and painstaking way. Certainly, by all logic, we can propose this possibility: all powerful He could simply have willed that all men know Him from their birth; yet He did not. His instruction to us is not offered in accordance with whatever "rules" are proper to His own way of knowing things. His revelation is offered in accordance with our own way of knowing; it is offered through sign and symbol, as we offer knowledge of ourselves to each other; it is offered through word and gesture, as we struggle to unfold the mystery of our own lives; it is offered with the same danger of misunderstanding, with the same threat of frustration which hangs over our attempts to communicate the truth.

In our Western tradition God has offered Himself to us by inserting Himself totally in the world in which we live. In creation He has left the signs of His presence. In creating us in His image He has opened the door for our approaching Him. In the history of Israel He has left the signs of His life. Finally, in Christ He has actually become one of us for the sake of speaking to us as we speak to one another, about the things that we can never tell one another. He has joined, once and for all, all the Truth of divinity with all of the weakness of humanity — except for the willful weakness of sin — and has radically changed humanity in the process.

The Western tradition of mysticism retraces

those revelatory steps. It commits itself to a unity with the world of nature, to a love of the being-in-the-body which is man's way of living, to a fascination with the Laws of God's creation. It makes these commitments in the belief that in them it will find the way back to the Lord.

But this is not the way of modern man. Modern man is overwhelmed by nature; he is overwhelmed by the technology he has developed for the control of nature; he is overwhelmed by the notion of sin, and he is unable to face it in himself. In spite of our brief flirtation with radical incarnationalism in the 1960's, man has now come full circle and identifies "religious experience" with ways and means of escaping the realities that oppress him. Modern man is much more in tune with a more Eastern style of mysticism, but an Eastern style as understood by Western minds. There is none of the genuine depth and subtlety of the true Eastern religious experience; there is only a sensationalism that follows from the mangled perception that the Eastern way is somehow "easier" than the Western.

If we can characterize the Western strain as "incarnational," we can call the Eastern "transcendental" or "ecstatic." Whereas the Western way insists that all knowledge comes through nature and then through the body, the Eastern maintains that knowledge of the truth only comes when we escape the shackles of nature and the body.

III. Martyrs, Monks, And Missionaries

Even though the lives and spiritual experiences of the Desert Fathers may be quite interesting and even inspiring, it is necessary for us to pose one very practical question: What value can all of this have for our own spiritual lives? If it were being suggested that real Christian living demands that we all flee to the desert, then the argument would be clear, if unacceptable. But since that extreme is not being suggested, we are left with the task of defining more precisely what relation the story of the Desert Fathers can have to us today.

We should begin this discussion with a very general comment: events or movements which change the life of the Church have a power which proceeds outward from a radical center and ultimately affects ordinary Christian people. The fact of martyrdom in the age of persecution, for example, changed the whole Church, but there were only relatively few people at the radical center of those events. In other words, only relatively few were actually martyred. Somehow the fact of martyrdom had a power which radiated outward, proceeding from the deaths of the few who were killed and affecting the lives and faith of the majority who survived. We believe that the same is true for the monastic movement in general: whereas relatively few people actually went out to the desert or to the monasteries, their radical commitment had a profound effect on the majority of Christians. In the same way, the missionaries of the sixteenth and seventeenth centuries were involved in a movement which profoundly changed the Church; the change was not only the obvious one of the growth of the Church through conversions, but also the more subtle change that took place in the lives of ordinary Christians who remained at home in Europe.

In each case — martyrdom, monasticism, and the missionary spirit — a small group of people involved themselves in a radically Christian activity, and the power of their activity strengthened the faith of the majority of Christians who did not engage in the same radical activity. In each case the activity was expressive of some deep need in the Church, and it outlined in stark and bold contrasts a road to holiness that was appropriate for a given age. We do not suggest that twentieth-century Christians should flee to the desert, but we do suggest that we, like the contemporaries of the Desert Fathers, can grow and benefit immensely by contact with their radical renunciation. We are suggesting that our needs today are remarkably similar to the needs of the age in which the Fathers lived, and that if we are willing to open our minds and hearts to their experiences, we can benefit as surely as their contemporaries did.

When we speak of a similarity of needs, we are speaking of two different things. First of all, there is a fundamental need which is shared by all generations of Christians; secondly, there are special needs that arise in particular cultural circumstances. The fundamental need shared by all generations is a need to attempt to reconcile the kingdom of God with the world in which we live. Each generation must face that problem or else lose its faith. If we pretend to solve the problem by maintaining simply that the "kingdom" and the "world" are separate and irreconcilable realities, then we spiritualize our faith to the point where it becomes unreal and unrelated to the problems of daily living.

On the other hand, if we attempt a simple solution based on the conviction that the kingdom is already completely present in our world, then we trivialize the faith and we risk killing it altogether. Theologians describe this as the problem of *eschatology*. A transcendent eschatology maintains that the kingdom is totally outside of this world and that we can know it only when we have finally escaped from our earthly prison. An immanent eschatology insists that the kingdom is already present here on earth and that we have the task of making that kingdom visible by our compassion and our works of charity.

You may already have seen that many of the

basic quarrels between Christians are rooted in this problem. "Faith" versus "Good Works," for example, is a problem which is simply one expression of the more fundamental eschatological question. If a person opts for a transcendent eschatology and believes that the kingdom is completely invisible and beyond man's experience, then he will believe that his salvation comes from faith alone. If, however, he chooses to accept an immanent eschatology and believes that the kingdom is at hand in the world around us, then he will believe that his salvation must be achieved through his good works, in his attempts to witness to the kingdom through his activities.

Gospel Sacrifice

Being a follower of Christ in any age demands sacrifice, and the willingness to be open to the call of the Gospels. In our own age, in spite of the hostility to faith which one may find, we have centuries of Christian tradition to support and encourage us.

Being a follower of Christ in those primitive days called for heroic sacrifice. It meant being scorned by one's neighbors; it meant living a life of severe moral purity; it meant literally giving all things up for Christ. As generations passed, however, and it became plain that Jesus did not intend to return immediately, the more subtle problems had to be faced. In the primitive Church, for example, after a person was baptized he could receive the Sacrament of Penance only once. Again, the thinking was that one surely could hold out in perfection for the short time that remained until Christ's coming. As time passed the practice of that sacrament changed, so that Christians could receive it more frequently as they struggled to work out their moral problems. If it was necessary to wait for the Lord for some time, then it would also be necessary to make a living in the world, and Christians would have to learn to apply the Gospel message to subtle questions of business ethics. If the Lord's coming was to be postponed, then men and women would have to learn to deal with their sexuality in a Christian way, and many subtle questions in this area would have to be faced.

The more complex and subtle the questions became, the more the spirit of urgency and heroism went out of Christianity. Being a follower of Christ no longer seemed so costly an affair; now it seemed to mean simply living as well as one could, struggling with the same problems everyone else had to face, and doing one's best to be conscious of gospel values in day-to-day living. Being a Christian was no longer so much a matter of radical renunciation as it was a question of learning to "make do" in an imperfect world — and what was there that was so new about that?

The fact of martyrdom in the age of persecution certainly addressed itself to this basic problem. Once again, the cost of Christian faith was clear: if one wished to follow Christ one would have to be prepared to make the ultimate renunciation, the same renunciation Christ had made Himself. One would have to be prepared to give up one's very life for the Faith. Now, not everyone was actually called upon to make that ultimate sacrifice. But that is not the point: martyrdom became the horizon against which ordinary Christians lived their lives. Even if only *some* Christians were being murdered for their faith, that fact raised profound questions for ordinary people. One would have to ask, "If there are those willing to die for the Faith, it must be a thing of infinite worth; am I living in such a way that this infinite worth is clear in my life?"

The age of martyrs produced many saints. Those who were martyred are the obvious saints. Not so obvious are the many more whose faith was challenged by the heroism of the few. These unknowns became saints not because they sacrificed their lives, but because the sacrifices made by others inspired them to live the Christian life more seriously and more perfectly. The radical witness of the martyrs revealed the true value of the Faith to them and moved them to convert themselves thoroughly to Christ.

In the age of the Desert Fathers, the same fundamental problem presented itself. Was the kingdom of God transcendent, a thing far off and out of reach, or was it near at hand, already present in the world? Like the saints who had gone before them the Fathers refused to be beguiled by any apparently simple answer. They knew that the real answer could only be found by a person who was willing to suffer for the kingdom, to work so hard that the immanence of the kingdom would be manifest, and to believe so deeply that the transcendence of it would be revealed. They knew that the real point was the *cost* of faith: the man willing to invest nothing of himself would receive nothing from the Lord.

Their flight into the desert and the radical renunciation which they lived were their personal route to holiness. In that total conversion they began to answer the eschatological question for themselves. Their actions and style of living also addressed themselves to a more contemporary problem, a problem rooted in their particular cultural situation. The acceptance of Christianity by the empire had made being a Christian easier than ever, and the comfort of that peace between Church and empire was dulling the faith all over the world. Now it seemed that being a Christian would cost nothing at all; in fact, it seemed that faith paid higher human dividends than unbelief.

The vast majority of Christians did not follow the Fathers into the desert, and yet their exodus changed the whole Church profoundly. The monastic movement which grew out of their flight to the desert nourished the faith of Europe for centuries. It presented a challenge and a high ideal which raised the level of belief, religious practice, and morality for all Christians. Their simple renunciation cut powerfully through all the subtleties of religion and reminded ordinary people that behind all the argumentation was the simple gospel challenge: "If anyone wants to be a follower of mine, let him renounce himself and take up his cross and follow me" (*Matthew 16:24*).

The missionary movement of the sixteenth and seventeenth centuries dealt with complex needs in much the same way. In fact, it combined the virtues of martyrdom and monasticism. The missionaries renounced the comforts of life in civilized Europe just as surely as the monks had, and they faced death and martyrdom in their work. Their activity was a way of approaching the eschatological question. Like the martyrs and the monks they understood that one could not pretend that the kingdom of God was a simple thing to be understood in one way or another. They were convinced that in order to find the kingdom, that "pearl of great price" (*Matthew 13:46*), they would have to renounce all things and follow Christ. Furthermore, their work addressed itself to a more contemporary problem of their cultural situation.

The religious wars and interminable quarrelling of the Reformation period had left Europe spiritually drained. The attention and imagination of common people were being captured by the great feats of exploration and discovery which were being undertaken for commercial and political reasons. The missionaries were men and women whose spirituality was vibrant and creative enough to see in their age a new opportunity for revitalizing the gospel life. They would renounce all things and thus work out their own salvation; in the process they would bring the Good News of the Gospel to people who had never heard it before.

Again, most Christians did not become missionaries; they did not leave the relative comfort of their homes; they did not face death at the hands of strange and unknown peoples. And yet the missionary spirit permeated Europe, and the heroism of the missionaries inspired ordinary Christians to commit themselves more totally and more deeply to the Faith. Once again the cost of faith had been made clear, and many who did not become missionaries were moved to reconsider their own lives and to convert themselves more completely to Christ and His way.

As recently as the last century, St. Thérese of Lisieux lived her short life as a sickly nun in a cloistered convent in France, yet she is known as the patroness of missionaries. Certainly she did not go on missions, and her title is not due simply to the fact that she prayed for the Church's missionary efforts. Her faith and her total gift of herself to the Lord flowed precisely from her being inspired by the missionary spirit: the spirit of total renunciation, of taking up the cross, and of devoting one's entire life to the Lord.

We believe that "desert silence" and the way of prayer that it inspires are meaningful in our world today because they underline the cost of the Faith, because they demonstrate the lengths to which some heroic souls were willing to go in order to live in the presence of God. We believe that their way of life can inspire new heights of faith in our age as surely as did martyrdom and monasticism and the missionary's zeal.

We believe that it is essential in our own age that the eschatological question be raised anew. Should we allow ourselves to be intrigued by esoteric spiritual movements which suggest that the kingdom of God is totally outside of our own world? Should we join the many who run after exotic Eastern spiritual cults in search of a disembodied state of nirvana? Should we commit ourselves to a hollow, falsified transcendence that sees salvation in drugs and the drug subculture? Should we ally ourselves so completely with the new Pharisees of our age that we, too, will renounce all institutions and cut ourselves off completely from the Church and her two-thousand-year history of searching for the Truth about the kingdom?

Or should we join that other camp that reduces spiritual value to social concern by insisting that the kingdom is here and now, not other-worldly? Would it be proper for us to "de-mythologize" Christianity so thoroughly that we are left alone with nothing but what is best in ourselves as we see ourselves now, and "make do" with what we consider our own best efforts today?

If we could drink in the spirit of the Desert Fathers, if we could borrow their way of prayer and all of the re-formation of self that leads to it, we could come to realize the cost of Christian faith. We could be awakened to the profound value that led them to the desert and we could commit ourselves to finding that same value in our daily lives. By coming to know their heroism and their radical sacrifice we could restore the sense of urgency to our own spiritual living and begin to approach a new kind of heroism in our own pursuit of the kingdom.

If we could come to appreciate their protest against the pointless luxury, the complacency, and the corruption of their own age perhaps we could see the same emptiness in our own. Instead of the mute and impotent protest of the man who *says* he abhors our age's lack of values and yet slips back into the mire of "going along," we might break through to a new personal strength rooted in the Gospel. Instead of the foolish cultism and faddishness of "health foods" and "ecology" and "sensitivity groups" perhaps we could rediscover the true center of our own being, our radical oneness with nature, and our proper place in God's nature and in His plan for creation.

IV. A Way Of Prayer

Prayer is not an activity or a project to be undertaken. Prayer is a state of consciousness within which the mind and heart are open to perceive the fundamental union which exists between God and the soul. So-called "methods" of prayer aim at disposing a person to this sense of union, but they can never create the union. Our union with the Lord exists because He has created us, because He has called us to be His, and because in Christ He is now gathering all things to Himself.

Although a great deal of active effort is required to arrive at it, true prayer involves a great degree of passivity and availability to the Lord. Real contemplation, for example, is not so much a matter of our contemplation of God as it is a matter of realizing that God is already contemplating us.* Disposing oneself to that consciousness, however, is a difficult and costly task. It involves cutting oneself free from all of the devices man in society has created to protect himself from the frightening questions of ultimate importance. If one is interested in locating those ultimate questions, we can suggest a simple starting point for the search. One can begin by honestly facing the issues that come into the mind in those last few minutes of consciousness before sleep. In those moments all of life's defenses and rationalizations slip away, and we are more or less naked with our most primitive fears and needs. What are some of the questions which most frequently spring to the mind in those moments? Here are a few: What will death be like? Will I cease to exist altogether after my death? Am I an honest person, or am I projecting a false image of myself? How much of a hold does sexuality have over me? Do I manipulate others for my own advantage? Do I allow my least noble parts to rule my life and affect all of my decisions? Am I a good person, or do I spend my life using and hurting others, ignoring God, and wasting my own energies in pursuit of impermanent advantage? Am I really loved, and have I allowed myself to love others deeply and unreservedly, or have I held back parts of myself, imagining that "the best is yet to come" and that the present is not worthy of my full attention? And, if this is true, will I someday find myself alone, unloved, and frustrated, with myself completely spent and with nothing to show for the

*See *Contemplative Prayer*, by Rev. Alan J. Placa; Living Flame Press, 1976.

effort of living?

Our way of living, in this or in any age, aims at making the present moment most comfortable and enjoyable. It aims at insulating us from the disturbing and deeply personal questions that can detract from our ability to enjoy life in the passing moment. The Desert Fathers sought to detach themselves from that insulation; they sought to face those most disturbing questions with their full consciousness rather than with the residue of energy left after the day's activity. They set out on that search convinced that if they could face the pain of their greatest fears and weaknesses they might also find their greatest hope and strength.

They began their search by facing their own sinfulness. They set out to examine their lives in utter honesty and in deep humility. Their self-accusation may sometimes seem brutal to us, but it brought them face to face with their own selfishness, their lies, their impurity, and their manipulation of others. Their remorse may seem morbid to us, but it was no more extreme than the excesses of rationalization to which they — and we — had gone to cover up sinfulness. Their hatred for their sins (some of them were great sinners, but most of them had only the ordinary failings of human living) was a powerful spiritual emetic which sent them into momentary convulsions of remorse, but ended by leaving them purified of both their sins and their efforts to overlook them.

They were convinced that their search for union with God was not a search for novelty, for something new and unheard of in human experience, but a process of returning, of renewing, of re-forming themselves so as to rediscover the union with God which had been in them all along. They knew that there was a fundamental union with God in themselves because they had been created in His image and likeness, and they knew that there was an intimate relationship of sonship because Christ had died for them, and they had been baptized into His redeeming death.

First they faced the truth about themselves, and then they tried to face the truth about the world around them. They operated out of the conviction that there is a natural order in the world, an order created by God, and that man has a specific place in that order. They believed that man had disassociated himself from that order by his personal sinfulness, his willful denial of his proper place in nature's order, and by protecting himself from nature's rhythms and cycles.

Having begun the process of purifying themselves of sin, they went to the desert to immerse themselves in nature's rhythms. They wanted to be part of the cycle of light and dark, to work and move in the light God had created for man and to take their rest in the peaceful darkness of His night. They wanted to break out of the human cycle of lighting up the night to make it seem like day and shutting out the sun's light to prolong sleep. They wanted to be part of the rhythm of light and dark which is implied in God's creation, not to recreate the world for their own need and pleasure.

They wanted to feel their dependence on nature's yearly cycle, receiving their food "in due season" (*Psalm 104:27*). They reinserted themselves into the year's rhythm of death and resurrection, sowing the seed in their small gardens, watching it die in the earth, anticipating its new life with fruit a hundredfold, and finally reaping its goodness for themselves.

In all things — in their personal morality, in their sanctification of the hours of the day and night, in their living by the pace and gifts of the year's seasons — they wanted to reconnect themselves to the world of nature, to the world of God's creation. And this discipline, this asceticism was no mere exercise: it aimed at liberating what was best in them; it aimed at disposing them to see the presence of God in the whole universe, in nature around them, and in their own souls.

Slowly and gradually, as their discipline grew and as their self-control increased, they felt confident enough to let themselves go, to give up control of themselves. They became convinced that they had freed themselves sufficiently from society's manipulative ways to trust themselves to move in the ways of God and of nature. If they sought solitude it was not because they despised the company of others, but only because they wanted to be alone to find God's company in nature and in their own purity of heart. If they formed communities of monks it was not because they were lonely, but because they felt the need for the encouragement and support of others engaged in the same task of finding the company of the Lord.

The only "method" of prayer they used was the recitation of the ancient psalms, in imitation of Jesus and His disciples at their Temple prayers.

They divided their vocal prayer into "hours," making that exercise a part of their overall plan to sanctify all of the hours of the day. They prayed when they arose with the sun. They paused in their work to praise God. They blessed their meals. They prayed to God for His blessing and protection before they slept. They woke to keep vigil in the night so that they would lose no opportunity to bless God's name and refocus their attention on the Creator-source of the rhythms they were rediscovering.

Their hours and vigils were not the sum total of their prayer, however. They were the self-conscious means by which they tried to kindle in themselves the sense of God's presence. They were the exercises they undertook to prepare themselves for prayer. Their prayer was the peace of heart that came from the realization that they were once more a part of God's creative plan, not rebellious elements of creation living as if there were no God and no plan for creation.

When asked to describe what they were doing and what they were experiencing in prayer, the Fathers never attempted to put those truths into words. They insisted that only those who had tried to pray and had finally come to some experience of the Lord's presence could truly know the peace which was their goal. The following story is told of the monk Theodore in the *Sayings* of the Fathers:

> "Another brother asked . . . Abbot Theodore, and began to question him and to inquire about things which he had never yet put into practice himself. The elder said to him: As yet you have not found a ship, and you have not put your

baggage aboard, and you have not started to cross the sea: can you talk as if you had already arrived in that city to which you planned to go? When you have put into practice the thing you are talking about, then speak from knowledge of the thing itself!"

If we trust the words of the Fathers and believe that they found deep peace and the presence of the Lord, then we must be willing to "find a ship," "put our baggage aboard," and "begin the crossing" to that city of life. But is it possible for us to find that prayer of union with the Lord without undertaking the radical abandonment of all things the Fathers undertook? The only possible honest answer is no. If we cannot find in ourselves the same spirit of remorse for sin, if there is in us no willingness to separate ourselves from the world's security and its devices, if we are not ready to renounce all things and to reunite ourselves with the rhythms of God's nature, then we can have no hope of praying as they did.

The further question is whether it is necessary to leave the world and flee to the desert in order to dispose ourselves to the union and peace they found. We believe that renunciation can be undertaken in the world. We believe that ordinary Christians can free themselves from the weakness of the world while still enjoying its sweetness. We believe that a man or woman living in the world can dispose himself to the sense of God's presence which came to the Fathers. Perhaps they could not have done it without their flight to the desert, but they did not have the advantage we have of knowing of their quest and their experiences. They were trailblazers who abandoned everything out of a deep faith that they could find spiritual peace. But they undertook their journey without real direction and without a clear idea of what their goal was. They only knew that they were going away from the world men had created for their own comfort and were rediscovering the world God had created for His own glory.

With that goal in sight, we can begin our journey here and now. We can find the "desert" in ourselves and commit ourselves radically to reordering our lives to put ourselves back into harmony with the natural order of God's creation. We can reform our moral lives so that they begin to conform to the laws of nature. We can use the blessings of technology with restraint and reflection so as to have them serve us in our quest for God, rather than stifle us in pursuing the Truth about ourselves and God. We can begin to free ourselves from what is trivial in our food, our dress, and our entertainment so as to rediscover what is essential.

We can treat the earth and our own bodies with new respect and honor, so that we can begin to see ourselves as part of what God has made. All of this is a way of prayer. If we can couple these disciplines with a conscious awareness of God, with regular habits of praying, with devotion to the Church and her sacramental life, then we can come to the "city" of peace the Fathers found. Our quest has to be this: to salvage man's technological mastery of the world so that it becomes progress toward union with the Lord rather than a self-serving flight from Him; to rediscover in society a source of encouragement and support rather than a crowd in which to hide from the Truth; to see the Church as the Body of Christ, as an inspiration to grow, as a source of the Food of life, rather than as an excuse for real religious living and real searching for the face of God.

Since prayer itself is not simply an activity to occupy a certain proportion of one's time, the improvement of one's prayer life cannot be a project to be undertaken. "Prayer" ought to be the proper name given to the whole process of growing in Christian life; it ought to be seen as the state of mind that evolves in those who are committed to re-forming their entire lives in harmony with God's will.

Prayer cannot be a goal in itself, unless one is willing to settle for only the appearance and routine of praying. Prayer must be the end product that arises spontaneously in the midst of a life that is gradually being returned to God. The prayerful person must be one who is making serious efforts on several fronts: in his personal morality, in his respect for his own body and its basic needs, in his attitude toward nature and its rhythms, in his relationship to the Church, which is the Body of Christ, and in his efforts to grow in understanding of God's Word and the Church's teaching and traditions.

If prayer is the heightened consciousness of God's presence in the soul, and if our separation of ourselves from the world of God and nature deadens our power to perceive that presence, then it is essential that our moral lives be re-formed in the image of God's order of creation. If a man's personal sinfulness consists of his being selfish and manipulative and insincere in his dealings with others, then he is disrupting the order of nature. He is separating himself from the purpose God had in giving man free will by using that freedom to manage and reconstruct reality in the image of his own desires, rather than using it to commit himself honestly to others so as to live in the image of the mutual love and commitment of the Trinity.

If a man's personal sinfulness consists of a looseness of sexual morality, then he is disrupting the order of nature. He is separating himself from the most profound purpose for which his body was created: that it should serve to express in honesty and love the deepest invisible feelings of the heart, not that it should become a man's possession, a thing apart from himself, and a toy for his pleasure.

If a man's life is marked with sin he will not be a prayerful man; he must first locate the weaknesses of will which are cutting him off from being taken up into God's life, and then he must repent of those weaknesses. The reform of life which is called for is more than a mere exercise in self-control; it cannot be a mere effort for moral perfection. His repentance is not a goal in itself, and it must be enlightened by a deeper purpose. The man who seeks to become prayerful must understand that sin alienates him from the natural rhythms of God's creation, and that this alienation will blind him to God's presence.

A man dedicated to growth in prayer must also see the role his body is meant to play in that growth. Our bodies are to fit rationally into the scheme of nature, into nature's plan for all physical things. If a man pampers his body and stuffs it with rich foods and drinks and pushes it to the limits of its endurance for the sake of making it into his personal vehicle for enjoyment, then he disrupts the order of nature by separating his body from its true environment. He creates a false world as a setting for his body's life, a life that is conceived of as independent from the life of the rest of the natural world. Rather than finding in his very physicality a sign of his own union with the whole of creation, he sees the body as holding him back from the achievement of supreme pleasure. He begins to bribe and coddle the flesh so as to draw it into his plan, rather than allowing it to reveal to him God's plan.

In the state of prayer a man senses the fundamental union of his whole being: the physical and the nonphysical parts of his being are one. It is only the man who is far from the Lord and far from prayer who sees the body as a prison, a trap which holds him back from his destiny. When a man makes the breakthrough to prayer he finds his real destiny in the being God created for him, the being-in-the-body which connects him intimately with the whole created universe and with its Creator. But, before that breakthrough can be achieved, the body must be purified of all that is meant to dull it, to insulate it from nature, and to force it to serve the mind as if the mind were some alien being.

This is the proper role of asceticism in Christian living: not to punish and subdue the body, but to liberate it from the willful attempt to disorient it, to turn it into a tool for man's own designs. Wholesome asceticism aims at returning the body to the purity God intended for it; it aims at reconstituting the possibility of harmony between body and soul, between man and his environment. The Desert Fathers did not go out to the wilderness to escape their bodies, but to return them to nature, to return them to purity and union with nature. They did that so that they could once again see their bodies as the home of a person seeking union with the Lord.

This purification of the body implies a new respect for the natural rhythms of the universe around us. The Desert Fathers achieved that respect in a radical way, putting themselves at nature's mercy completely. They developed a respect for the seasons of the year, for example, because their supply of food depended radically on the weather and the seasons. They had only the most primitive methods of heating, and no means of cooling except the desert breezes. With their radical sensitivity as a spearhead, we can grow in our awareness of nature's cycles without abandoning what technology has given us for our protection. If a hurricane is brewing, a man need not walk out in it and risk his life; on the other hand, he should not retreat blindly into a climate-controlled cocoon which no sign of nature's power can penetrate. Recently, when a hurricane struck Long Island, we and the priests of our house watched its fury. We were safe and protected, and yet we could feel nature's power and get a sense of our proportional place in the physical world. As the eye of the storm passed over us, we walked outside and sensed the ominous stillness, the tense quiet of the trees already bent by the first winds and now waiting for yet another attack.

We experienced our own smallness and frailty. That great storm could have picked us up and snapped us like so many twigs. It had already cut off our electric power so that we were without light or air-conditioning or the mesmerization of the television which could have turned the personal experience of the storm into an impersonal "media event." And the experience of our frailty was mixed with a clearer perception of our own strength. Our house was constructed well enough to save our lives, and the potential destruction had drawn us together in conversation and relaxation such as cannot be programmed or scheduled. Just that smallest openness to nature had released a natural congeniality we rarely see in ourselves. In a similar way, a more thorough sensitivity to nature's rhythms can dispose us to see more of what is natural in us; ultimately, it can do what it did for the Fathers: it can open us up to see the presence of God deep within us and within nature. It can lead us to the state of prayer.

Finally, one more re-formation is necessary. Just as a man must re-form his moral life around the order of nature, just as he must reinsert his body into its natural environment, just as he must renew his sensitivity to nature, so must he reawaken his openness to the Church as the Body of Christ. If we were to use only the terms we have been developing thus far, we could define the Church simply as a community of prayer. The Church should be the congregation of those who are in the process of rediscovering their union with the Lord.

One thing the Church definitely must *not* be is a community of those who have despaired of ever really finding the Lord and have settled for their meetings as a substitute for real prayer. The German theologian Karl Rahner has said that the Church is most perfectly herself when she is celebrating the Eucharist. In the few moments of that celebration we are each drawn out of the worlds we have constructed to isolate and protect ourselves and drawn into the presence of Christ. In that sacramental moment the Lord offers us the reality of His presence surrounded and supported by the signs of His life in Scripture, preaching, song, and common devotion. That celebration ought to be the summary of all the moments in which we have successfully sensed our union with the Lord and with each other in our daily living. It ought, furthermore, to be an inspiration to commit ourselves more deeply to the style of living which will bring us the knowledge of that union more deeply each day.

The Church's sacraments and teachings exist so that we can be supported and encouraged in our efforts to re-form our lives. They exist as a reminder that we are not alone in the task, that it is the power of Christ and His initiatives which draw us to prayerfulness. They exist so that we may perceive that we are known and loved as individuals but that we are saved as a community, as the People of God. We are not cut loose, wandering in loneliness looking for hidden truths. We are members of Christ's Body; the Truth "is near" to us "on your lips and in your heart" (*Romans 10:8*).

V. The Desert "Way" Of Prayer

When we subtitled this book "A Way of Prayer for an Unquiet Age" we did not mean to suggest that we would propose a simple, magic formula for prayer that would raise us all immediately to the level of heroism which marked the lives of the Desert Fathers. There is no such magic, no such formula. It is part of the essence of Christianity that all "easy ways" are shunned.

Have you ever considered how simple it would have been for the all-powerful God of the universe to have saved us and revealed Himself to us? With a simple act of His will He could have seen to it that each man and woman born into the world would be born with a complete understanding of all spiritual reality. With a simple act of His will He could have forgiven all our sins and restored us to the first innocence of the day of creation. But He did not. He created man in freedom, and He worked His salvation and His revelation in a painstaking and time-consuming way that respected our freedom and our intellects and our way of knowing and learning. He does not ordinarily communicate with us in a "divine" way, by flashes of sudden insight or gifts of immediate knowledge. More frequently He has shown Himself in sign and symbol, in the events of Israel's history, in the words and gestures of Christ which were so often misinterpreted and ignored, in the history of the Church which is filled with the holiness of the saints and with the faults and failings of lesser men and women.

If there is any particular divine "pedagogy" or teaching method it is this: to teach in a way that is proper to the learner. It has been God's purpose in all of history to address man in a language which he can understand and to offer man the *opportunity* to choose God over his own will.

This was the primary insight of the Desert Fathers: that the secret of God's will was written in the world He had created, and that only a man who had learned to be perfectly silent could ever come to read that secret. They sought an exterior silence as a setting for their search for interior silence. The interior silence they hungered for was the quelling of the voices of weakness and lust and selfishness and dishonesty that live within man's heart.

Certainly they had a method of praying. They prayed according to the oldest tradition of prayer: they prayed from the Book of Psalms. Those earthy, sometimes violent, and always deeply moving songs were the perfect expression of the rediscovery of the human spirit which they sought. They sang those inspired songs, they read the Scriptures, they treasured the words of the great Spiritual Fathers, and they meditated in silence. They turned over in their hearts their own feelings of remorse for their sins. They contemplated the peace of God's all-encompassing presence. They shed tears of sorrow and, finally, tears of joy. But all of their prayers were only the expression of their *way* of prayer. Their *way* was to seek the Lord in all things, to face the truth about themselves and about the world around them, to reintegrate themselves into God's creation and His holy Law.

The Psalms rose from their lips as naturally as they had from David's own lips. They had reunified themselves with the Spirit of the Lord, and so they prayed in the words of that Spirit.

In this short section we will describe a way of using the Psalms which has been developing over the whole two thousand years of the Church's history. We urge you to attempt this form of prayer and to integrate it into your quest for the silence of God's desert.

SANCTIFYING THE HOURS OF THE DAY

The single most ancient and continuous tradition of prayer in the Christian Church is the praying of the Psalms at various fixed hours of the day. Certainly the Desert Fathers prayed this way; the *Sayings* of the Fathers are full of references to the regular schedule of psalmody which they observed each day. We know from the Gospels that Jesus and His disciples followed the Hebrew tradition of praying from the Psalms each day, and the Acts of the Apostles tell us that the apostles went to the Temple each day for some form of prayer.

Over the centuries a very rich body of prayer has grown up around the core of the hundred and fifty Psalms. The "Divine Office" or "Breviary," originally the prayer book of monastic communities and more recently the official prayer of all priests and deacons in the Roman Catholic Church, is the fruit of these centuries of development. In this form of liturgical prayer the day is divided into five "hours" or "offices" of prayer: "Morning Prayer" to begin the day, "Daytime Prayer" to sanctify the working hours, "Evening Prayer" as darkness falls, and "Night Prayer" before retiring. The fifth prayer is the "Office of Readings" and is built around several Psalms and the meditative reading of passages from the Scriptures and the great Christian writers.

There is a basic structure which is common to all of these "hours" of prayer. Each begins with praise of God in an ancient liturgical hymn which is appropriate either to the hour of the day or the season of the year. The theme of praise is continued in a selection of several Psalms which form the heart of the prayer. A selection from Scripture is included and a short period of meditation on the reading is invited. Each hour also includes prayers of petition for the Church, the whole world, and the needs of the individual or community offering the prayer. Night prayer includes a short examination of conscience or penance ritual, and the Office of Readings has longer selections from Scripture and the Fathers of the ancient Church.

If treated only as a formula of prayer this "Liturgy of the Hours" can become a meaningless ritual, but when properly integrated into a growing spiritual life and a sensitivity to the "desert silence" we have been describing, it can be a rich and highly imaginative source of prayer. The notion of sanctifying the hours of the day and night with a regular and well-integrated round of praise and petition so captured the imaginations of simple ancient Christians that they were anxious to imitate the monastic practice. The Rosary as we know it, with its fifteen "mysteries" of ten prayers each, has its roots in the efforts of simple lay people to unite themselves in prayer with the sanctity of the monks' life.

Using the simple prayers they knew by heart, ordinary Christian people imitated the sanctification of the hours which characterized the monks' prayer life. The hundred and fifty Psalms were mirrored in the hundred and fifty "Hail Mary's" of the Rosary. The fifteen "Our Father's" are short Scripture readings interspersed through the prayer. The Apostles' Creed is a symbol of union in faith with the whole Church. The "Hail Holy Queen" is a song of liturgical praise of God for His goodness to Mary. Finally, the repeated "Glory be to the Father," or Small Doxology, carries the primary theme of praise through the entire devotion.

The illiterate people of those ages joined themselves in prayer to those who had renounced everything to follow Christ. Housewives used piles of one hundred and fifty beans or pebbles to count off their prayers in imitation of the number of the Psalms they could not read. As time passed, the familiar chaplet of beads became a handy device for counting these rhythmic prayers.

The key to authentic use of the Liturgy of the Hours is integration: the method cannot stand alone; it must be integrated into a life-style which values the order of God's universe. The peasants of the early Middle Ages who imitated the Liturgy of the Hours were people of the land, farmers who lived in tune with God's nature and its ways. They were well integrated in the Church as their primary society. They held firmly to simple and straightforward moral values. This rhythmic prayer of the hours was an expression of their closeness to the natural order of things in the rest of their lives; it was a device by which their consciousness was raised to perceive the presence of God in their lives.

We must be cautious in recommending this form of prayer. The danger is one we have already mentioned: that a form of prayer may be substituted for prayer itself. What we are commending to you is the *way* of prayer of the desert, and that *way* is not equal to any method. It is an attitude of silence, a posture of openness to creation, a profoundly peaceful recognition of God's presence which comes to men and women who have committed themselves to personal reformation. Any "method" of prayer can only serve to heighten our consciousness, to establish a setting for spiritual openness, and to focus our attention on God, who is the source of the order and real silence of the universe.

This method should only be undertaken simultaneously with a multi-faceted attempt to restore one's own personal harmony with God's creation. It must be accompanied by a sense of repentance for sin and serious moral conversion, a sincere attempt to discipline the body's wants so as to rediscover its natural needs, a reawakening of appreciation for the world of nature, and a recommitment to the essential nature of membership in the Church and use of her sacraments and teachings. When integrated into this larger project of personal conversion to the Lord, this method can *lead to* real prayer.

The last chapter contains a summary outline of some suggestions for use of this method. We include the basic outline of each hour of prayer and some suggested Psalms and Canticles which are appropriate to each hour. We also include one or two lines from each Psalm so that you may have the flavor of that selection.

If you find this method useful, you may wish to expand these selections with favorite Psalms and readings of your own, or to refer to one of the versions of the Breviary which are now available commercially.

VI. Meditations On The Sayings Of The Fathers

The Fathers of the Desert broke their silence only to encourage one another and to share what they had learned from the Lord in their contemplative silence. The *verba*, or sayings of the Fathers, are their words of wisdom and holiness passed down from master to disciple all over the desert places where they made their simple homes.

In the long run, one grasps the spirit of these remarkable men best by sampling these sayings that served to initiate others into the holiness and devotion of their lives of asceticism and prayer.

THE LIVES OF THE FATHERS

To speak of "biographies" of the Desert Fathers is almost a contradiction in terms. The whole point of their going to the desert was to have their lives hidden in God. In fact, we know very little of the details of their lives, except that they had an immense impact on the Church and on society for many centuries. We know that their wise and pointed sayings are revered to this day as marvelous summaries of Christian asceticism and spirituality.

Any biography at all, in the modern sense, is quite impossible when considering the great, but rather solitary lives of the Desert Fathers. Modern men seek to uncover all of the pertinent facts and dates that can possibly be gathered. But how can such details be gathered from the lives of men whose main goal in life was simply to secure the salvation of their souls at any cost? Their seemingly fanatical quest for spiritual perfection demanded a measure of solitude and anonymity which makes ordinary biography impossible.

But, even in their solitude, they were generous men. They were willing to share the one thing which they valued: their silence, their hidden life, their search for the face of God. Most of the "hermits" of the desert allowed younger men to share their dwelling places with them. They worked and prayed with these young brothers, and they shared with them the fruits of their own prayer and reflection on the Gospels. The "cells" in which they lived were small cottages in the deserted regions of Egypt into which they had travelled. Often these "cells" were nothing more than caverns in the rock. They kept small vegetable gardens near their cells, and they raised whatever food they might need.

The "master-disciple" relationship of the elder and his young companions seems strange to us. The master seemed to be chiding and correcting his protégés constantly. In fact, the elders must have loved their disciples as gifts from the Lord, given to them so that they themselves might grow in the process of sharing their spiritual growth with others.

The relationship was a very impermanent one, in that the younger man was expected to move on and establish himself as an "elder" for the training of others who would come to the desert. In this way, the wisdom and experiences of many generations of holy men were available to each newcomer. Their life was harsh by our standards; their work was hard and fatiguing, and their hours of prayer were long and perhaps even tedious. And yet, in the simple consolation they offered one another, in their shared quest for holiness and salvation, they supported and encouraged one another and they inspired many others to follow them.

THE SAYINGS OF THE ELDERS

The best approach to biography in this case is to offer to you the only true record that exists: that is the record of the words of the Fathers* passed down from generation to generation. In the few pages that follow, we offer selections from these sayings and some meditations in the spirit that we have caught from them. We hope that this sampling

* *Sayings of the Fathers*, translated by Alan J. Placa.

will inspire you as the Fathers have inspired us and that it will whet your appetite to survey the rich literature which is available on the desert experience.

ON HUMILITY

Then, Lord, who can be saved?

True Christian humility is not a psychological state of mind; it is an attitude of the heart. Humility ought not to be rooted in a belittling of the self; it ought to find its roots in this recognition: that the one thing of value which we all possess has come to us as a free gift from another, and that one thing of value is the hope of salvation.

When the Lord Jesus told the story of the rich young man who turned away in sorrow from the invitation to follow the Master, the disciples did not miss the point of the story as we often do. There is a certain cold terror in their question, "Then, Lord, who can be saved?" and that terror comes from their realization that it is not only the poor who will find entering the kingdom a difficult task. What is more, the Lord's answer offers very little consolation at first: "For man, this is impossible." Our hope and consolation are in His next words: " . . . but for my heavenly Father all things are possible."

The world makes of humility a very negative thing. A popular musical play some years ago had in it the line "It's not the earth the meek inherit; it's the dirt!" The Christian who is making his way to the kingdom in silence and in prayer, however, understands humility in a way that goes far beyond such superficiality. Humility is a sense of our belonging to God, and not to ourselves, that springs out of the depths of the converted soul. To be humble is a distasteful thing when it is understood as some sort of exercise imposed from outside of a man so that he can accomplish some goal. But it is not really that at all. Humility is not part of some abstract definition of what a person *ought to do* in order to become a Christian; it is a most sensitive description of what a man does in fact feel when he has become a Christian.

A very popular saying among the Fathers of the Desert was, "Who am I?" They offered that in response to those who sought wise and holy words of them; they offered it as a response to those who sought their judgment on moral questions; and they offered it to those who claimed they had come to the desert in search of holiness. Who *are* we that we should counsel, or support, or encourage one another? More fundamentally, who are we that we should be invited into eternal life by God?

Love, freely given, is a humbling power. In the first rush of love, when we are overcome by the fact that someone can find us lovable, we are often filled with joy at our new-found or newly confirmed attractiveness. But when love becomes truly deep, we are humbled by the immensity of the gift that is love. When another human being can offer his or her entire life to us, we are brought face to face with the realization that *no one* is worthy of such a gift. It is precisely in its being a free gift that it is liberating and affirming and, at the same time, humbling.

The free gift of God's love, the free gift of salvation and eternal life, the gift of Christ's life-blood freely poured out for us — all of these liberate and affirm us and at the same time they draw humility up from the very roots of our being. To be so deeply loved when it is so thoroughly unearned is a great mystery, always. And, always, it recreates us and makes us aware of our own nothingness. But beyond that, this same humility moves us to love more deeply, to offer ourselves more completely, and to share what we have experienced of the gift of love with others.

"Abbot Alonius used to say, 'Humility is the land where God wants us to go to offer Him sacrifice.' "

Lord, it is to the empty place inside of myself that I long to go. It is to the place, the desert uninhabited by men, where You have made Your dwelling place within me that I long to go. In my own nothingness I find the richness of Your free gift of love, and in that very nothingness I find the profound value of my life: that I am loved.

* * *

"One of the elders was asked what humility was, and he answered, 'Humility is forgiving a brother who has hurt you before he comes to ask pardon for himself.' "

Lord, the power of Your forgiving love is alive in us. Let us not keep it pent up inside, but rather let it flow from us. Let it reach out, in humility and love, to our brothers and sisters who live still with the burden and anxiety of their sins. Let us be Your instruments of hope and salvation for the world. Give us this humility always.

* * *

"One of the brothers asked an elder, 'What is humility?' The elder replied, 'To do good to those who do evil to you.' Then the brother asked, 'What if a man cannot go that far; what should he do then?' The elder answered, 'Then let him get away from those who do evil to him and keep his mouth shut.' "

Lord, when my own weakness is so great that I obscure Your forgiving power, free me from my own anxiety and from my thirst for self-righteousness. Let me go my way in peace, and at least not be a scandal and a stumbling block to those who have not yet found Your light.

* * *

"Once, in the Valley of the Cells, a feast was being celebrated, and the brethren were eating together in their gathering place. There was one brother present who called out to the one who was waiting on tables and said, 'I do not eat any cooked food; I only take a little salt to season my dry bread.' So the waiter called out to another brother in the presence of the whole assembly and said, 'That brother there does not eat cooked food. Just bring him some salt.' When he heard this, one of the elders went to the brother who only wanted some salt and said to him, 'It would have been better for you if you had stayed at home and eaten your fill of meat alone in your cell than to allow this thing to be heard in the presence of so many brethren.' "

Father, give us strength to do Your will in silence and humility. Just as our salvation is Your free gift, given in the silence of our own souls, so will our consolation be in the quiet peace of Your love. Let us not parade our good works before men, seeking the consolation of their praise, when we know that only Your love brings us life everlasting.

* * *

"One of the elders told the story of another elder who was working diligently in his cell and wearing a hairshirt when Abbot Ammonas came to visit him. When Abbot Ammonas saw the hairshirt, he said, 'That thing will do you no good at all.' But the elder said, 'Three thoughts are troubling me. The first impels me to withdraw somewhere into the wilderness. The second impels me to find a foreign place where I am known by no one. The third impels me to wall myself up in this cell and to see no one and to eat only every other day.' Abbot Ammonas said to him, 'None of these will do you any good, either. Instead, sit in your cell, eat a little bit each day, and always have in your heart the words which the Publican says in the gospel story.* In this way you can be saved.' "

*The reference here is to the Jesus prayer, "Lord Jesus Christ, Son of God, have mercy on me, a sinner!"

Father, open our eyes to see that it is never by our own efforts that we are brought to peace and salvation. It is only Your loving power and forgiveness that offer us eternal life. We glory in our weakness and in our sins, because they are the occasion for Your power to be felt in our lives; they are our nature's invitation to You to pour out Your life and grace on us.

* * *

"One of the elders said once, 'If you see a young monk climbing up into heaven by his own will, grasp him by the foot and throw him to the ground! What he is doing is not good for his soul.' "

We know that if our goals are in sight, if the treasure we seek is within our grasp, then the Lord may give us the unkindest blessing of all: He may grant us the goal we have set for ourselves. Like the Publican in the Temple, we should not even know what we need. We should know only that we need God's love and mercy to attain goals we cannot even dream of! Father, have mercy on our impatience; fill up our longing with Your peace. Make us one with You and with one another in seeking Your will and Your promises!

Love the Lord . . . with your whole mind

The mind of man is an exquisite instrument, the most exquisite ever created. When one considers the depths of triviality to which the mind is lowered and the preposterous and pompous "heights" of convoluted pseudo-intellectuality to which it is forced to float, one can lose sight of the fact that the mind is a primarily functional instrument. It has a purpose to serve in the project of making man's life in the world more livable, more human, and more liberated. The mind is man's servant, not his master. But the man who has discovered no true integrity in himself, the man who has discovered no "self" capable of using the gift of the intellect, imagines that reason is his highest gift. It is not. "Logic circuits" can be produced by the millions on chips the size of postage stamps. "Imagination" and "creativity" can be simulated by electronic control mechanisms. Man's highest gift is his humanity, and it is that gift which links him to God. It is man's vocation to integrate *all* of his other gifts by coming to experience his own being, and in that experience of himself as the unique, human part of God's creation he begins to find the Lord.

Exquisite instruments always bring out the worst in man, for some reason, but they also open him up to the best in himself. The automobile, for example, ought to be a device which helps man to be liberated. It ought to provide him with mobility and independence. And yet it has already become an instrument of destruction. Used unwisely it kills people directly; used unimaginatively and selfishly it destroys in a more subtle way by its pollution and its waste of our resources.

At one end of the spectrum there is the person who uses his car selfishly for commutation, sitting paralyzed on a public highway alone in his car, while thousands upon thousands of others sit paralyzed and alone in theirs. The unimaginative and selfish among us have turned this potential instrument of liberation into a device for further isolation and alienation.

At the opposite end of the spectrum are those who have cut the automobile loose completely from its function. They race automobiles, or customize them, and in countless other ways make the automobile an object of man's attention and devotion in itself.

The same extremes are present in the ways men have come to use the gift of intellect. For the unimaginative and selfish the mind is only an elaborate signalling device for avoiding pain and discomfort. It turns a man in on himself and acts as a further barrier to new experiences and to growth. For the trivial among us, the mind has become an object of attention and devotion. The entertainment value of the intellect has completely overcome *its* functionalism. There is an important place in life for mental games, for crossword puzzles, and for logical riddles, but the solution of these trivial diversions is not the mind's function.

The proper object of man's mind is that which is tantalizing in its complexity. The proper object of man's mind is that which is lovable in its being.

Every intellectual process which *ends* in knowledge is a wasted process. The true goal of all our thinking and our knowing must be *love*. The power of the intellect ought to resolve itself, finally, in man's heart, not in his head. The "output" of the mind, to borrow the barbaric jargon of the computerized world, ought not to be new babbles of words; it ought to be a new conformity of man to the Truth of God's love in the world.

"Two brothers went to visit an elder who lived alone in Scete. One of them said, 'Father, I have learned all of the Old and New Testaments by heart.' The elder said to him, 'You have filled the air with words.' The other brother said, 'Father, I have copied out the Old and New Testaments and keep them always in my cell.' To this the elder replied, 'You have papered over your windows with parchment.' He went on, 'But do you not know the One who said, "The kingdom of God is not in words, but in power"? and again, "Not those who hear the Law will be justified before God, but those who live it out"?' So the brothers asked him what was the way of salvation, and he said to them, 'The beginning of true wisdom is the fear of the Lord and humility with patience.' "

Lord, we give You thanks for the gift of our intellect. We ask You to liberate us from all excesses in the use of our minds. Make us unselfish, so that our minds will be open to new experiences. Give us integrity of heart so that we may never lose sight of the purpose for which You have blessed us with intelligence. Let us love Your Word in Scripture not for itself and not for its mere content, but for the gift of Your life which it imparts.

* * *

"A certain philosopher asked St. Anthony, 'Father, how can you be so happy when you are living here deprived of the consolation of literature?' Anthony replied, 'My book, philosopher, is the nature of the things God has created. Any time I want to read the words of God, that book is always before me.' "

Open our eyes to the wonders of Your creation, Lord. Make our minds attentive to the Truth which lies hidden in the life and being of all Your creatures and all the elements of Your creation. Do not allow us to become slaves of the mind's smallest powers, but rather, let us learn to unleash its grandest force, its ability to make us one with all of Your world.

* * *

"A brother went to Abbot Theodore and began to question him and to ask about things which he had not yet experienced or put into practice himself. The elder said to him, 'As yet you have not found a boat, and you have not put your baggage aboard, and you have not yet begun to cross the sea. How can you speak as if you had already arrived at the place you are planning to go to? When you have put into practice the things you talk about so well, then you will be able to speak out of your own knowledge of the thing itself!' "

Lord, do not make us traders in words! When the mind races ahead of our experiences, let that be a lesson in humility to us; let it drive us to seek new experience and new love of Your Truth which is in the world You have created. Never let our curiosity lead us to idle chatter, and protect us from the emptiness in ourselves and in others which leads men to speak as if they have known and loved and suffered what they have never known outside the small confines of their own minds.

* * *

"Abbot Pastor once said, 'If you have a chest full of clothing and you leave it closed up for a long time, the clothing inside of the chest will rot. It is the same with the thoughts in our hearts. If we do not carry them out by physical action, after a long while they will spoil and turn bad.' "

Lord, free us from the temptation to muse idly over what we have learned and thought. Free us from the lethargy of too much speculation, and make us men and women alive with love and anxious to serve You and our brothers and sisters with the power of the Word we have heard and learned.

* * *

"One of the elders said, 'When an ox or a mule has his eyes covered, he can be made to go around and around turning a mill wheel; but if his eyes are uncovered, he will not go around in the circle of the mill wheel. In the same way, if the devil manages to cover a man's eyes, he can humiliate that man in every kind of sinning. But if a man's eyes are not closed, then he can easily escape from the devil.' "

Lord, let us love learning and the power of the mind, for it is a road to freedom for the life of man. To know the world and its ways, to be familiar with the experiences of other human beings — these are the first steps to living in peace and integrity of heart. Bless us with a hunger for this learning always!

* * *

"Abbot Palladius said, 'The soul that wants to live in harmony with the will of Christ should either learn faithfully what it does not yet know, or else teach openly what it does know. But if, when it is free, the soul desires neither of these things, then it is afflicted with a kind of madness. For a distaste for learning is the first step away from God and a lack of the hunger for those things which are proper to the soul in search of God.' "

Lord, our hunger for You leads us to want to know You and the world You have made. Our growing knowledge of the Truth leads us to love You more deeply and to desire You more profoundly. Let us love learning, let us love Your Word in Scripture and the "book" of the nature of Your creation, so that we may ever grow in love.

"One of the monks, a man named Serapion, went out and sold his book of the Gospels and gave the money to those who were hungry. He said, 'I have sold the book which told me to sell all that I had and give it to the poor.' "

Lord, lead us always to unlock the power of Your Word. Let it seep into our souls and make us men and women of faith and action. Let our knowledge of Your Word lead us to deeper love of Your world. Make us instruments of Your plan to save and reconcile all things to Yourself in Christ.

ON EASE

My peace I give to you

Where is the source of our peace in the world? Where is the center of our being, the place we look to in order to discover whether or not we are well-integrated parts of the reality of the world? Men and women in the world look outside of themselves, to external things, for their ease and peace of mind. They look to their homes and possessions, to their position in their professions, and to their public standing in their communities. They are ill at ease until all of these externals conform to someone else's image of how a person ought to live and look in the world.

If the source of our ease is in external things, in material things and in our appearance before men, then all of our good works are soured and trivialized by being fitted into a preconceived "movie script" version of the "good life." Whatever goodness a man in the world is able to achieve is converted into empty self-adornment. And furthermore, it is adornment of a "self" over which we have no personal control: it is a "self" predefined by the standards of the world, not the true self buried deep within the person and given its real hope of peace by the Lord.

The Christian person turns to the Lord living within him, and within the Church, as the source of peace. As the world has the power to convert even my good works into nothingness because it robs me of peace, so the Lord has the power to turn even my weaknesses into peace by His power of forgiveness and His hope of life.

"Abbot Pastor said, 'Just as smoke drives bees away from their hives and allows their honey to be stolen from them, so a life of ease drives the fear of the Lord out of a man's soul and takes all his good works away from him.' "

Lord, defend our eyes from the blindness that the substanceless smoke of worldly ease causes. Give us clarity of vision and purity of heart to see You as the source of our real peace.

* * *

"Abbot John said, 'A monk must be like a man sitting under a tree who looks up and sees all sorts of snakes and wild animals charging at him. He sees that he cannot fight them all off, and he climbs the tree and escapes their attacks. The monk should do the same at all times. When evil thoughts are aroused by the enemy, he should turn in prayer to the Lord, and then he will be saved.' "

Lord, You are our true refuge. Those who place their hope and their trust in external things have no defense against their own weakness. For us, You are our hope. Your loving forgiveness makes strength of our weakness by making of our fears the invitation to prayer and to security in Your peace-giving presence.

ON SILENCE

Be still, and hear the Lord

Silence is often the greatest teacher of all. How much we learn from the person who has the confidence to be silent in the presence of others. How shallow and filled with fear is the relationship which can never bear a moment of silence.

In the presence of those whom we do not know and love we produce a flood of words and noises to fill the empty void of our own fear of not being accepted. We listen halfheartedly, looking for the opportunity to speak, to "keep the conversation going." There is no silence because there is no peace, no confidence that in our love of one another we can value one another's silent mutual gift of self.

Some men and women deal only in words, not in realities. They are so busy speaking of love that they have no time to offer themselves in love to another person or to the Lord. They are so anxious about speaking of faith that they have no strength left to throw themselves into the Lord's arms in loving belief in His goodness.

True conversion and true re-formation of the self means reorganizing our entire lives around the quest for silence and peace, for confidence in ourselves, in other men and women, and in the Lord.

"Theophilus of holy memory, who was Bishop of Alexandria, travelled to Scete. When the community assembled, the brethren said to Abbot Pambo, 'Say a word or two to the Bishop, that he may be edified in this place.' The elder answered, 'If he is not edified by my silence, then there is no hope that he will be edified by my words.' "

Lord, bring us always to those whose lives speak eloquently and teach profoundly by their silence and peace. Let us love ourselves so much, because of Your love for us, that we will offer to others the consolation of Your love and the promise of Your gift of peace and life.

* * *

"Once a brother came to Abbot Theodore of Pherme and spent three days begging him to speak a word to him. The Abbot, however, did not answer, and the brother went away sad. Then a disciple said to Abbot Theodore, 'Father, why did you not speak to him? Now he has gone away sad.' The elder answered, 'Believe me, he is a trader in words, and I spoke no word to him because he seeks to glory in the words of others.' "

Lord, give us the gift of silence. Let us not be anxious to cover ourselves with words so as to defend our nothingness with empty sounds. Lead us to confidence in Your love and in the love of our brothers and sisters, so that our words may be words of encouragement and faith and our silence may be the sound of the peaceful heart.

ON BEARING INSULTS

Give him also the other cheek to strike

People immersed in the life of the world fight what often seems a never-ending battle against institutions and individuals who threaten them. Each man carves out for himself his own tiny kingdom of security and battles off any and all who challenge his position there. On a grand scale, nations live in fear of one another; they expend their creative energies in monitoring the words and actions of the leaders of other nations, alert for any insult or belittling of their own national honor. In homes and in families men and women of the world, fearful that they will be unloved or forgotten or esteemed too little, quarrel with those they love most in self-destructive efforts to protect the affection and loyalty to which they feel entitled. The Christian who has turned his back on that world and begun to walk into Christ's kingdom has a new security, a new peace in his heart. The man who senses attackers on every side is the man who sees himself as the center of the universe. He interprets every word and action as directed at him and as potentially threatening to his being and value in the world. The Christian who has sought the Lord in the quiet of his own heart, who has entered the desert place of his own spirit, bears insult and hurt with a new strength.

Are we so insecure and prideful as always to believe that the one who insults us has found some secret fault in us? Doesn't the Christian understand that we all share the same human weaknesses and that the insultor could become the victim of his own cruelty as easily as the one insulted? Perhaps the root of the insult is not in my weakness, but in the weakness of the one who offers the insult. Perhaps, more deeply, the root of all insult and hurt and meanness is in the human condition of which we are all so terribly afraid.

The Christian seeks to purify his heart of the false tenderness which makes him ever alert to insult, so as to soften his heart to hear and understand the Truth of God's love and of His promises. The root of my true value in the world is God's love for me, not my power to overcome the insults of others.

"Abbot John used to tell this story. Once there was a disciple of a Greek philosopher whose master ordered him to give money to everyone who insulted him for three years. When this period of testing was completed, the master said to him, 'Now you can go to Athens and learn wisdom.' When the disciple entered Athens he met a certain wise man who was sitting at the gate insulting everyone who entered and left. He also insulted the disciple, who immediately began to laugh. 'Why do you laugh when I insult you?' said the wise man. 'Because,' said the disciple, 'for three years past I have been paying money to those who insulted me, and now you offer me the same for nothing.'

'Enter the city,' said the wise man. 'It is yours!' When Abbot John told the story he would say, 'This is the door of God, by which our fathers, who rejoiced in many tribulations, entered the City of Heaven.' "

Lord, show us the way to Your heavenly city. Show us the narrow path that leads to salvation, and protect us from our urge to travel the crooked and selfish ways of our pride. Purify our hearts of selfishness and of false self-esteem. Make us pliable to Your will and forgiving of those who offer insults out of their own fear.

* * *

"Abbot Anthony taught Abbot Ammonas in this way: he said, 'You must advance further in the fear of God.' And he took him outside the cell and showed him a stone, saying, 'Go and insult that stone, and strike it over and over again.' When this had been done, Anthony asked Ammonas if the stone had answered back. 'No,' said Ammonas. St. Anthony said, 'Then you, too, must reach the point where you no longer take offense at anything.' "

Lord, put into us hearts of "stone" to protect us against the small, self-deluding rages of the world, and give us hearts of gentle flesh open to Your words of encouragement and forgiveness. Teach us to fear no man's words, but to have in our vision always the fear of Your power.

"There was a certain brother who was praised by the whole community in the presence of Abbot Anthony. When the elder examined this brother, he discovered that he could not bear being insulted. The Abbot Anthony said, 'You, brother, are like a house which, though it has a large and strong gate, is entered freely by thieves through all its windows.' "

Lord, we so often build up a strong gate to defend ourselves against the impotent insults of a world which cannot harm the soul, and in our frantic efforts to save face and build up human respect, we leave ourselves open to the weaknesses that crop up from within. Give us Your strength, give us Your peace, so that in Your presence we may be truly secure and serene.

ON THE POWER OF TEMPTATION

You must be tested, like gold in the fire

In the world, people strive for the day when all their struggles will end. They deceive themselves, dreaming of riches and power as a guarantee that they will have peace and face no more challenges or threats to themselves. The world, sadly, gives them the answer to their prayer in the stillness of death.

We Christians are not growing towards the day when there will be no struggle; death is not our goal: our goal is life! We are growing towards the day when we can face the realistic struggles of human living with serenity and security which are rooted in the Lord and in His gifts to us.

To feel the Lord's power at work in us through our prayer and through the ministry of His Church makes our moments of trial and temptations become the occasions for our deepest growth in self-knowledge and freedom.

Only the fool seeks to be free of trial and struggle. The wise man, the man of the Lord, strives for the strength to face temptation courageously and hopefully. He strives to know himself in the tests the world gives and to find his freedom to live in the real world, full of trials, with joy and confidence in the Lord.

"Abbot Pastor used to say, 'A monk's virtue is made visible by the temptations he endures.' "

Lord, make us courageous in facing trials. Lead us to choose life with all of its struggle. We are in the world, and the world is the only place where our salvation can be worked out by Your power. We turn to You, not to be delivered from temptation, but to be delivered from the evil that grows in our hearts when we fail to face our trials with courage and confidence in You. Draw us near to You, make us lovers of the world which You have made, and lead us to discover our own freedom as Your children by facing the world, with its best and its worst gifts, as our home.

* * *

"Abbot Pastor said that Abbot John the Dwarf had prayed to the Lord and the Lord had taken away all of his passions so that he became completely impassible. Having achieved this, he went to one of the elders and said, 'You see before you a man who is completely at rest and no longer experiences temptation.' The elder said to him, 'Go and pray to the Lord and ask Him to cause some struggle to be stirred up in you, because your soul can only mature in struggles.' When the temptations started up again, Abbot John did not pray that the trial be taken away from him, but rather he only said, 'Lord, give me strength to get through the fight.' "

Lord, make us anxious to face the world. Let us know that in the world are all the opportunities for our growth and for our failure. Show us that the man who avoids failure also denies himself growth. We face the temptations of life bravely, confident that Your help and power are available to us. We are confident, also, that when we fail You are near to us to forgive, to raise us up, to encourage, and to give us new confidence to begin again in the way of growth.

ON DYING

Death, where is thy sting?

When a man's whole life is lived as a battle against a world in which he feels he is an alien, then death is the greatest terror of all. The man who has no interior life is faced daily by a thousand small defeats, a thousand insignificant ways in which time and space and the elements get the best of him. All of these forces of nature are his enemies and, in the end, nature itself will overwhelm him by decomposing the body he lived in and for.

But the Christian does not live "in" the body, nor does he live "for" the body. The Christian lives *through* the body. He senses his essential unity with the whole of the created universe. Death holds no real terror for the Christian because it is one of the definitions of his earthly life: it defines him as an integral part of the constantly perishing universe. But Christ's death and resurrection define him as the *unique* part of the universe which is reborn in its apparent decay.

"An elder said, 'A man who keeps death before his eyes at all times will at all times overcome his cowardice.' "

Lord, let us be thoroughly transformed in Christ; let us be always imbued with the hope of His resurrection. Let us have a sober fear of death joined to an understanding that our death defines our earthly life and limits our earthly possibilities but also begins the mystery of our eternal life with You. Open our hearts to this truth: that in the moment of our death we shall have exercised all of our options, made all of our choices, and our earthly life will be an organic whole, complete in Your sight. With that image of death before us always, let us live in the light and in the hope of our resurrection, so that when we come to the hour of death we may present to You a life lived courageously, marred by sin but full of our striving for perfection. Make us ready, in that last hour, to present ourselves confidently before the throne of Your mercy.

"An elder saw a certain brother laughing and said to him, 'In the presence of the Lord of heaven and earth we shall have to answer for our whole life, and you can laugh?' "

Lord, give us the gift of seriousness and a strength of purpose as we face our life's trials and choices. Give us joy without superficiality, give us pleasure without foolishness, so that we can love our life dearly and yet not cling to it. Make us strong and full of life here on earth, so that we may come at last to the fullness of life after death.

* * *

"They tell the story of one of the elders who was dying in Scete. The brethren surrounded his bed, dressed him in the burial shroud, and wept for his death. But he opened his eyes and he laughed. He laughed again, and then a third time. When the brethren saw this, they asked him, 'Father, tell us why you laugh while we are weeping?' He answered them, 'I laughed the first time because you are afraid of death. I laughed the second time because you are not ready to face death. And I laughed the third time because I am leaving behind my labors and going to my rest.' As soon as he had said this, he closed his eyes in death."

Our Lord and brother, Jesus Christ, has passed through death and risen to new life. Confident because of His victory, let us cleanse ourselves of the unreasonable fear of death and be prepared always to meet our Father. Let us live each day as if it were our last by finding in it all of its goodness, all of its potential for growth and for love. Let us lay ourselves down to each night's rest confident that we have lived life to the full in this day and are prepared to meet the Lord in His kingdom should He call.

ON THE GOAL OF THE HIDDEN LIFE

Why not be totally changed into fire?

How quickly the world teaches all of its children to reach only for the attainable! How sad it is that man's imagination has been reduced to a toy to be played with only in idle hours! We Christians are a people called to see many visions and then to laugh at them all. We are called to know that whatever we can grasp, whether by the mind or the imagination or even by our own spirit, is as nothing compared to what God has in store for us in His kingdom.

If humility could flourish in our souls, if we could learn to deal faithfully and creatively with our temptations, if we could remove ourselves from the world's frantic race for ease, if we could even overcome our fear of death itself, we would still be an eternity away from the peace and happiness our Father has prepared for His children.

The contemplative spirit, the spirit of the desert, is the spirit of fire. It is the consuming light of this knowledge: that God has known us, has grasped us, and is calling us to lay our cares on Him alone. Our Father waits in patient love for our response to His gifts. When, finally, we offer ourselves to Him, He shares with us the purifying fire of His own vision of the world He has created.

"Abbot Lot came to Abbot Joseph and said, 'I keep my rule of life, I fast, I pray and meditate, and I maintain a contemplative silence. I do all of these things as well as I can in my own small way. As far as I can, I try to cleanse my mind of unwanted thoughts. Now, what more should I do?' The elder stood up to answer, and he stretched out his hands towards heaven, and his fingers became like ten lamps of flame. He said, 'Why not be totally changed into fire?' "

VII. Liturgy Of The Hours: A Prayer Method

1. The Invitation to Prayer

At the beginning of the day's prayer, the traditional invitation to prayer, Psalm 95, is recited. This Psalm is a call to give praise to the Lord:

> *"Come, let us sing joyfully to the Lord; let us acclaim the Rock of our salvation."*

Normally, the day's prayer would begin with Morning Prayer, but if for some reason this is not so, this invitation is recited before whichever hour begins the prayer of the day.

2. The Office of Readings

We describe the Office of Readings first because it has no definite place in the sequence of the hours. In some ways it is the turning point of this entire method of prayer because it attempts to combine the rhythmic prayer of the Psalms and Canticles with the meditative, contemplative prayer that flows from reflective reading of the Scriptures and the works of the great spiritual writers. The mood of this hour is quiet and reflective, and it ought to be prayed at a time of day appropriate for peaceful meditation. Because it includes longer readings and invites longer reflection, it will be the longest of the prayers of the day.

(a) **Opening**

The traditional opening for all of the hours of prayer is:

"God, come to my assistance,
Lord, make haste to help me.
Glory be to the Father, and to the Son,
and to the Holy Spirit;
As it was in the beginning, is now, and ever
shall be, world without end. Amen."

(b) **Hymn**

Even when praying alone the singing of a short hymn at each hour is appropriate. Music has power to create mood, and singing brings us out of our private worlds to come into step with rhythms and paces outside of ourselves. We suggest no particular hymns, but leave that choice to each person's taste. We do, however, suggest that the hymns be appropriate either to the hour of the day (e.g., "Morning Has Broken" for Morning Prayer), or the day of the week (e.g., "On This Day the First of Days" for Sundays, or eucharistic hymns for Thursdays), or the season of the Church's year (e.g., "O Come, O Come, Emmanuel" for Advent). Alternatively, the hymn might express the mood or needs of the individual or community offering the prayer.

(c) **Psalms and Canticles**

We suggest any of the following as being appropriate for the Office of Readings; three short Psalms or parts of longer Psalms are usual at this hour:

Psalm 1: *The two ways of living:*
"Happy the man who follows not the counsel of the wicked
Nor walks in the way of sinners, nor sits in the company of the insolent,
But delights in the law of the Lord, and meditates on his law day and night."

Psalm 2: *The Messiah is King and Conqueror of the whole universe:*
"Ask of me and I will give you the nations for an inheritance
and the ends of the earth for your possession."

Psalm 3: *Our safety is in the Lord:*
"When I call out to the Lord, he answers me from his holy mountain."

Psalm 6: *A cry for mercy:*
"Have pity on me, O Lord, for I am languishing."

Psalm 9: *A thanksgiving for victory:*
"I will give thanks to you, O Lord, with all my heart;
I will declare all your wondrous deeds."

Psalm 10: *A prayer for help:*
"Why, O Lord, do you stand aloof? Why hide in times of distress?"

Psalm 12: *Prayer for help against oppressors:*
"Help, O Lord! for no one now is dutiful; faithfulness has vanished from among men."

Psalm 18: *Thanksgiving for salvation and victory:*
"You have given me your saving shield; your right hand has upheld me, and you have stooped to make me great."

Psalm 35: *The Lord can save us in persecution:*
"Let not my unprovoked enemies rejoice over me."

Psalm 131: *Childlike trust in God:*
"I have stilled and quieted my soul like a weaned child."

Psalm 132: *God's promise to David's house:*
"The Lord swore to David a firm promise from which he will not withdraw."

(d) **Readings**

Each day there should be two readings: one scriptural, one nonscriptural. One possibility is to read through a certain book of Scripture, one chapter each day. A book by a spiritual writer could be read in similar short, daily selections.

(e) **Reflection**

The readings should be followed by a period of silent reflection and prayer.

3. **Morning Prayer**

Morning Prayer should be filled with joy and hope and praise of the Lord. People's daily routines differ, but Morning Prayer should be celebrated as close to the beginning of the day's activities as possible. The overriding theme is praise of the Lord. We rejoice that the gift of life has been renewed this day. We rejoice in the sunrise and the signs of nature's awakening. We dedicate the day's work to the Lord and ask His blessing.

(a) **Opening**

(b) **Hymn**

(c) **Psalms and Canticles**
Choose the equivalent of three short Psalms, for example:

Psalm 5: *A morning prayer for help:*
"To you I pray, O Lord; at dawn you hear my voice;
at dawn I bring my plea expectantly before you."

Psalm 24: *The Lord enters His temple:*
"Who can ascend the mountain of the Lord?
or who may stand in his holy place?"

Psalm 29: *God's voice in the storm:*
"The voice of the Lord is over the waters
the God of glory thunders,
the Lord, over vast waters."

Psalm 33: *Praise for God's continual care:*
"Our soul waits for the Lord,
who is our help and our shield."

Psalm 36: *The malice of sinners, the goodness of God:*
"Sin speaks to the wicked man in his heart;
there is no dread of God before his eyes."

Psalm 47: *The Lord is King:*
"All you peoples, clap your hands,
shout to God with cries of gladness."

Psalm 48: *Thanksgiving for deliverance:*
"Great is the Lord and wholly to be praised
in the city of our God."

Psalm 51: *The prayer of repentance:*
"Have mercy on me, O God, in your goodness."

Psalm 57: *Morning prayer in affliction:*
"Awake, o my soul; awake, lyre and harp! I will wake the dawn.
I will give thanks to you among the peoples, O Lord."

Psalm 63: *Thirsting for the Lord:*
"O God, you are my God whom I seek; for you my flesh pines and my soul thirsts like the earth, parched, lifeless, and without water."

Psalm 100: *A joyful song entering the Temple:*
"Sing joyfully to the Lord, all you lands;
serve the Lord with gladness;
come before him with joyful song."

Psalm 117: *Praise for God's loving compassion:*
"Praise the Lord, all you nations."

Psalm 149: *The joy of God's holy people:*
"Sing to the Lord a new song of praise in the assembly of the faithful."

Exodus 15:1-18: *A hymn of victory after crossing the Red Sea:*
"I will sing to the Lord, for he is gloriously triumphant."

1 Chronicles 29:10-13: *Glory and honor to God alone:*
"Yours, O Lord, are grandeur and power, majesty, splendor, and glory."

Tobit 13:1-8: *God afflicts us only to show us mercy:*
"He scourges and then has mercy; he casts down to the depths of the nether world and he brings up from the great abyss."

Judith 16:1-17: *God our Creator cares for us:*
"A new hymn I will sing to my God.
O Lord, great are you and glorious, wonderful in power and unsurpassable."

Isaiah 45:15-25: *People of all nations will praise our God:*
"Turn to me and be safe,
all you ends of the earth,
for I am God; there is no other!"

Jeremiah 30:10-22: *The happiness of a redeemed people:*
"You shall be my people,
and I will be your God."

Daniel 3:52-90: *Nature's grand hymn of praise to God:*
"Sun and moon, bless the Lord;
praise and exalt him above all forever."

(d) **Reading**
A reading of one or two verses of Scripture follows the Psalms and Canticles. This may be a verse from a book one is currently reading, or a favorite verse.

(e) **Quiet Reflection**

(f) **The Canticle of Zechariah** *(Luke 1:68-79)*
"In the tender compassion of our God the dawn on high shall break upon us."
This canticle is always part of Morning Prayer. As the day begins we join Zechariah in looking forward to the work and salvation of Christ which lies before us.

(g) **Petitions**
Here we pray for the needs of the whole Church, of our country and the world, our families and friends, and ourselves.

(h) **The Lord's Prayer**

4. **Daytime Prayer**

This is a very short prayer, meant to come in the middle of the day's activity. Its purpose is to draw us back from what we are doing and to provide the perspective of faith. The Psalms deal with the difficulties that may arise in the course of a day, and they also focus attention on the Law of God as a reminder that we are to be true to Him in our day's work.

(a) **Opening**

(b) **Hymn**

(c) **Psalms**

Three very short Psalms or selections from Psalms are used at this hour, for example:

Psalm 7: *An appeal to God's justice:*
"O Lord, my God, in you I take refuge; save me from all my pursuers and rescue me."

Psalm 13: *A lament in sorrow:*
"How long shall I harbor sorrow in my soul, grief in my heart day after day?"

Psalm 14: *The foolishness of sinners:*
"The fool says in his heart,
'There is no God.' "

Psalm 17: *Save me, Lord, from those who hate You:*
"From you let my judgment come;
your eyes behold what is right."

Psalm 19: *Praise God for His Law of love:*
"The law of the Lord is perfect,
refreshing the soul."

Psalm 25: *Prayer for help and protection:*
"To you I lift up my soul,
O Lord, my God.
In you I trust; let me not be put to shame."

Psalm 26: *Trusting prayer of the innocent:*
"Do me justice, O Lord! for I have walked in integrity,
and in the Lord I trust without wavering."

Psalm 28: *A song of entreaty and thanks:*
"Hear the sound of my pleading, when I cry to you, lifting up my hands toward your holy shrine."

Psalm 34: *God is the Savior of the just man:*
"When the afflicted man called out,
the Lord heard,
and from all his distress he saved him."

Psalm 118: *A song of joy for salvation:*
"In my straits I called upon the Lord; the Lord answered me and set me free."

Psalm 119: *The praise of God's Law:*
"Happy are they whose way is blameless,
who walk in the law of the Lord."

(d) **Reading**

(e) **Quiet Reflection**

5. **Evening Prayer**

Together with Morning Prayer this is the most solemn of the hours. As Morning Prayer praises God for the night safely passed and asks His blessing on the day ahead, so Evening Prayer thanks Him for the day's work and praises Him for the gift of the peaceful evening to come. The hour is filled with praise and thanksgiving; it takes its pace from the quiet rhythm of the night. It blesses God for His saving power and looks forward to the everlasting peace of His kingdom.

(a) **Opening**

(b) **Hymn**

(c) **Psalms and Canticles**

Three Psalms or sections of Psalms or Canticles should be chosen from the following and similar selections:

Psalm 11: *God's unfailing support of the just:*
"The Lord is just, he loves just deeds; the upright shall see his face."

Psalm 15: *Who is worthy of God's presence?*
"O Lord, who shall sojourn in your tent? Who shall dwell on your holy mountain?"

Psalm 16: *The Lord Himself is our heritage:*
"I say to the Lord, 'My Lord are you. Apart from you I have no good.' "

Psalm 20: *A prayer for the king's victory:*
"May he send you help from the sanctuary, from Zion may he sustain you."

Psalm 21: *Thanksgiving for the king's victory:*
"He asked life of you: you gave him length of days forever and ever."

Psalm 27: *God stands by us in our distress:*
"The Lord is my light and my salvation: whom should I fear?"

Psalm 30: *The Lord delivers us from death:*
"O Lord, my God,
I cried out to you and you healed me."

Psalm 32: *The happiness of the forgiven sinner:*
"Many are the sorrows of the wicked, but kindness surrounds him who trusts in the Lord."

Psalm 41: *Thanksgiving for the Lord's healing:*
"Once I said, 'O Lord, have pity on me; heal me, though I have sinned against you.' "

Psalm 46: *God is our refuge and strength:*
"Come! behold the deeds of the Lord, the astounding things he has wrought on earth."

Psalm 110: *The Messiah is King and Priest:*
"The Lord has sworn, and he will not repent: 'You are a priest forever.' "

Psalm 114: *God delivers His people from Egypt:*
"Before the face of the Lord, tremble, O earth, before the face of the God of Jacob."

Psalm 141: *A prayer in time of danger:*
"Let my prayer come like incense before you; the lifting up of my hands, like the evening sacrifice."

Psalm 142: *The Lord is our salvation:*
"Lead me forth from prison, that I may give thanks to your name."

Romans 11:33-36: *All glory to God:*
"How deep are the riches
and the wisdom and the knowledge of God!"

Ephesians 1:3-10: *God's plan of salvation:*
"To bring all things in the heavens and on earth into one under Christ's headship."

Philippians 2:5-11: *Christ has been poured out for us:*
"At Jesus' name
every knee must bend."

Colossians 1:15-20: *All things were created through Christ and for Him:*
"He is the image of the invisible God,
the first-born of all creatures."

Revelation 5:9-10: *A redemption hymn:*
"With your blood you have purchased for God men of every race and tongue."

Revelation 12:10-12: *The judgment of God:*
"Now have salvation and power come,
the reign of our God and the authority
of his Anointed One."

Revelation 15:3-4: *The power and holiness of God:*
"O King of the nations!
Who would dare refuse you honor?"

Revelation 19:1-8: *Condemnation of the sinners and glory of the Church, the Bride of Christ:*

"This is the wedding day of the Lamb;
his bride has prepared herself for the wedding."

(d) **Reading**

(e) **Quiet Reflection**

(f) **Mary's Canticle:** "The Magnificat" (Luke 1:46-55)

"All ages to come shall call me blessed."

As evening comes we join Mary in thanking God for the demonstration of His power. She was rewarded for her humility, obedience and faith by the gift of being the first to follow Christ into the glory promised to all who believe. We aim to imitate her quiet prayerfulness and, finally, to share in eternal life.

(g) **Petitions**

(h) **The Lord's Prayer**

6. **Night Prayer**

This short prayer thanks God for His goodness during the day and begs for His protection from the evil symbolized by the darkness of night. The prayer should be simple; if possible it should be learned by heart so that it can be prayed as one falls asleep. As we retire for the night we briefly review the day and beg God's forgiveness for our faults and our failures to imitate His love and His gift of self.

(a) **Opening**

(b) **Examination of Conscience**
This should be a brief review of what has happened during the day, with special emphasis on facing honestly our sins during the day.

(c) **Hymn**

(d) **Psalms**
Night prayer should have no more than one or two short Psalms; Psalms like the following would be appropriate:

Psalm 4: *A song of confident thanksgiving:*
"Know that the Lord does wonders for his faithful one; the Lord will hear me when I call upon him."

Psalm 16: *God is my portion and my inheritance:*
"You will not abandon my soul to the nether world, nor will you suffer your faithful one to undergo corruption."

Psalm 31: *Trustful prayer in adversity:*
"Be my rock of refuge,
a stronghold to give me safety."

Psalm 86: *A poor man's prayer in time of trouble:*
"Keep my life, for I am devoted to you; save your servant who trusts in you."

Psalm 88: *A prayer in sickness:*
"My eyes have grown dim through affliction; daily I call upon you, O Lord; to you I stretch out my hands."

Psalm 91: *Safe in God's sheltering care:*
"With his pinions he will cover you, and under his wings you shall take refuge."

Psalm 130: *A cry for mercy:*
"Out of the depths I cry to you, O Lord; Lord, hear my voice!"

Psalm 134: *Night prayer in the Temple:*
"Lift up your hands toward the sanctuary, and bless the Lord."

Psalm 143: *A prayer in distress:*
"Hasten to answer me, O Lord, for my spirit fails me."

(e) **Reading**

(f) **Quiet Reflection**

(g) **Simeon's Canticle** *(Luke 2:29-32)*

When the infant Christ was presented to him in the Temple, holy Simeon felt that at last he could rest: he had seen the holiness of God. At the end of a day lived in God's presence we, too, can rest peacefully.

Living Flame Press
Locust Valley, N.Y. 11560

Desert Silence:
A Way of Prayer
for an Unquiet Age
by Rev. Alan Placa
and Rev. Brendan Riordan $1.75

" . . . And I Will Fill This House With Glory"
Renewal Within a Suburban Parish
by Rev. James A. Brassil $1.50

Book of Revelation:
What Does It Really Say?
by Rev. John Randall, S.T.D. $1.75

Praying With Scripture in the Holy Land:
Daily Meditations With the Risen Jesus
by Msgr. David Rosage $2.25

Source of Life:
The Eucharist in Christian Living
by Rev. René Voillaume $1.50

In God's Providence:
The Birth
of a Catholic Charismatic Parish
by Rev. John Randall $1.50

Contemplative Prayer:
Problems and an Approach
for the Ordinary Christian
by Rev. Alan Placa $1.75

Reasons for Rejoicing:
Experiences in Christian Hope
by Rev. Kenneth J. Zanca $1.75